Praise for *The Go-To Expert*

▐▐ Differentiating yourself from your peers is the challenge that every professional faces. This book gives you the clarity, process and confidence to make yourself stand out in a crowded marketplace.

TONI HUNTER, PARTNER, GEORGE HAY CHARTERED ACC...

▐▐ Just reading the contents list was enough to con... book that any professional or small business owner nee... book gives you the stuff that most books on networking... foundation to win business regularly from your network. Highly recommended.

CHARLIE LAWSON, NATIONAL DIRECTOR, BNI UK & IRELAND

▐▐ I thought I was pretty good at this 'expert' stuff and being noticed – until I read this! Packed with tips, I was left with a page full of things to do, and I genuinely believe that any professional will benefit from reading (and using) this book.

CARL READER, DIRECTOR, DENNIS & TURNBULL CHARTERED ACCOUNTANTS AND STRATEGIC ADVISERS

▐▐ Having become the Go-To Expert for raising your profile, Heather has shown she walks her talk. This book is a great guide for people who want to follow in her footsteps and learn how to sell themselves as the expert in their field. Buy it now!

JENNIFER HOLLOWAY, AUTHOR OF *PERSONAL BRANDING FOR BRITS*

▐▐ This book was made for you. More than just another 'How To' guide, if you take the message and wisdom to heart, then your future is set to develop in a rich and rewarding way. Of course, you will have to work diligently on your craft and get ahead. But if you love what you do, then that's easy.

JULIAN SUMMERHAYES, BLOGGER AND PROFESSIONAL SPEAKER

▐▐ This book is full of really helpful and practical tips for those wanting to succeed in business. I was taking notes before I had finished the first chapter.

JAMES MENDELSSOHN, CHAIRMAN, MSI GLOBAL ALLIANCE

▐▐ An excellent practical guide for everyone in professional services. If you want to move your career on, shifting from being just another professional advisor to being truly recognised as a Go-To Expert, this book will show you the way.

RICHARD NEWTON, AUTHOR OF *THE MANAGEMENT BOOK*

▐▐ With job security no longer a given, every professional needs to understand how to build up a profile and reputation in the competitive legal landscape – read this book and learn how to thrive whether you are employed, freelancing or doing interim work.

SHIREEN SMITH, LLM SOLICITOR AND PRINCIPAL, AZRIGHTS SOLICITORS

▐▐ This book proves to be a brilliant tool to help professionals appreciate the benefits of becoming recognised as the Go-To Expert in their field. The book gives you some truly great ideas on how to differentiate yourself from your competitors along with guidance on how to implement these ideas, whilst also embracing the social media methods of marketing.

CAROLINE BIRD, DIRECTOR, MENZIES LLP

‖ Like so many lawyers struggling to come to grips with the new environment in which we work and the increased need to find my own instructions, I have a shelf full of books which claim to point me in the right direction. Although my intentions are good, I've only ever managed to get through a few of them due to the fact that they have an alarming tendency to be full of buzzwords and light on specific advice on which steps to take to start changing your fortunes right away.

The Go-To Expert has no such problems. It is written very much as a 'business case' in its own right and not only equips you with the tools you need to succeed in our new multi-platform world, but explains why each step is important and how it can ensure your survival and prosperity. It can be dipped in and out of to deal with a specific point or worked through (as I did) to take you through the process of making yourself truly stand out for all the right reasons. With helpful case studies to demonstrate how the suggested steps have worked for others and a straightforward prose style and tone which doesn't leave you feeling baffled or indoctrinated, this is most importantly an easy and worthwhile read and is a sound basis for pretty much any personal development plan. And, if you don't have a personal development plan, this book will tell you why you should.

The Go-To Expert covers every base you'll need to set yourself apart from the competition and, to be honest, you can't afford to ignore it.
STEVE KUNCEWICZ, HEAD OF IP AND MEDIA, BERMANS LLP

‖ This is an essential and significant resource for anyone looking to develop their careers or their business, jam-packed with practical ideas to help you achieve that 'Go-To Expert' status.
PAUL HICKMAN, PARTNER, MENZIES

‖ *The Go-To Expert* is a great guide for aspiring professionals and reflects the changing world in which we operate. It is no longer good enough to be a very solid practitioner – you now need to be known for something and if that is as unique as possible so much the better. That isn't just about career progress to the highest level your skills can take you, it may just be about keeping the job you've got.
PETER GILLMAN, EXECUTIVE CHAIRMAN, PRICE BAILEY

‖ In our cluttered, competitive world of business, the fight for air time and mind space is fierce. Making somebody think of you first when they need what you do is a major marketing objective. Unfortunately few entrepreneurs or professionals get it right, which is why they struggle to market themselves, their ideas and their companies. As a fellow bestselling author on the topic of reputation and standing out in a crowd, I love what Heather Townsend has done with this book. It addresses the 'tyranny of choice' by explaining in very practical ways the benefits of becoming the go-to-expert, the power of niching and how to become irresistible to your target market. Using a blend of methods including the three massive reputation builders, writing, speaking and networking, she unpacks the mystery surrounding why some people get chosen and some don't. If you want to become the stand out option in a competitive environment, this brilliant book should be your blueprint of choice!
ROB BROWN, AUTHOR OF *HOW TO BUILD YOUR REPUTATION*

‖ Heather Townsend's *The Go-To Expert* provides a brilliant step-by-step guide to growing your professional services business. If you leave this book on the shelf you will miss out!
MATT BIRD, FOUNDER, RELATIONOLOGY

The Go-To Expert

The Go-To Expert

How to grow your reputation, differentiate yourself from the competition and win new business

Heather Townsend and Jon Baker

PEARSON

Harlow, England • London • New York • Boston • San Francisco • Toronto • Sydney
Auckland • Singapore • Hong Kong • Tokyo • Seoul • Taipei • New Delhi
Cape Town • São Paulo • Mexico City • Madrid • Amsterdam • Munich • Paris • Milan

PEARSON EDUCATION LIMITED

Edinburgh Gate
Harlow CM20 2JE
United Kingdom
Tel: +44 (0)1279 623623
Web: www.pearson.com/uk

First published 2014 (print and electronic)

Pearson Education is not responsible for the content of third-party internet sites.

ISBN: 978-1-292-01491-3 (print)
       978-1-292-01494-4 (PDF)
       978-1-292-01492-0 (ePub)
       978-1-292-01493-7 (eText)

British Library Cataloguing-in-Publication Data
A catalogue record for the print edition is available from the British Library

Library of Congress Cataloging-in-Publication Data
Townsend, Heather.
  The go-to expert : how to market and sell yourself to win business / Heather Townsend and Jon Baker.
    pages cm
  Includes index.
  ISBN 978-1-292-01491-3 (pbk.)
  1. Consultants--Marketing. 2. Specialists. 3. Expertise. I. Title.
  HD69.C6T69 2014
  001--dc23
                            2013046463

10 9 8 7 6 5 4 3 2

18 17 16 15 14

Cover design by David Carroll & Co
Print edition typeset in 10.25/14pt Frutiger LT Pro by 30
Print edition printed and bound in Great Britain by Henry Ling Limited at the Dorset Press, Dorchester DT1 1HD

NOTE THAT ANY PAGE CROSS-REFERENCES REFER TO THE PRINT EDITION

Contents

About the authors

Heather Townsend helps professionals become the Go-To Expert. She is the author of one of the top selling FT Guides – *The FT Guide To Business Networking*, the co-author of *How to Make Partner and Still Have a Life* and a high profile member of the professional services industry. Over the last decade, Heather has worked with over 300 partners, coached, trained and mentored over 2000 professionals at every level of the UK's most ambitious professional practices.

Heather is a member of the professional speaker's association. She regularly speaks at large conferences within the professional services sector e.g. ICAEW's insolvency practitioners conference. In 2011 and 2012 Heather judged the British Accountancy Awards.

Heather is increasingly gaining a reputation as a fresh thinking, astute, practice management expert. She regularly writes for the trade press and is often quoted in the national press. She writes monthly for CCH, a large software provider and technical publisher for the accountancy industry.

Jon Baker specialises in helping small professional practices grow profitably and sustainably from 5 to 50 people. He has 25 years' experience of managing, training and coaching in business helping ambitious professionals improve their leadership, marketing and sales skills. He is also an in demand speaker, social media and sales trainer (Jon is a member of the professional speaker's association). Before Jon started his own practice as a coach, he spent 17 years working for BP. In the last 7 years he has coached hundreds of business owners, helping to grow their firms by more than 63 per cent. He has also had blue chip clients; including BP, Total, and Feel Good Drinks.

Authors' acknowledgements

Thank you to everyone we interviewed for, or featured in, the book: Tim Luscombe, Gavin Hinks, Alan Stevens, David Kaye, David Stoch, Carl Reader, Martin Bragg, Adrian Jenkins, Guy Clapperton, Rob Brown, Sonja Jefferson, Sharon Tanton, Simon Chaplin, Lee Frederiksen, John Cassidy, Brian Inkster and Shireen Smith.

We'd both like to thank the team at Pearson and our amazing chief organiser, Lisa Bremner, for helping to make this book happen.

PUBLISHER'S ACKNOWLEDGEMENTS

We are grateful to the following for permission to reproduce copyright material:

Figure 4.2 from Infographics by Angie Phillips, ANG Creative Design; Figure 4.3 from Rob Brown at **www.therobbrown.com**; Figure 15.1 from Optima at **www.optimaabr.com/prophet**

In some instances we have been unable to trace the owners of copyright material, and we would appreciate any information that would enable us to do so.

Foreword

Countless books have been written about how to do networking, lead generation, social media, selling and brand management. Probably even more have been written about content mastery and how to become really good at doing something. Call those perspectives marketing and content, respectively.

Curiously, I can't think of any books that specifically link those two perspectives for <u>professional services –</u> how to develop and run a business built around the idea of expertise. Until this book.

It sounds so simple: <u>get better than anyone else at something and then build your business around it.</u> For example, we've all heard the quip, 'Build a better mousetrap and the world will beat a path to your door.' But that optimistic formulation begs a few critical questions.

The first is – why mousetraps instead of bicycles? If mousetraps, then what does 'better' mean? Is a green mousetrap better – or is colour irrelevant? How can I be better than anyone else at it? These kinds of questions go on, and on, and on.

The second question is – just how is it that people will come to beat a path to your door? How will they know where your door is? How beaten does the path have to be in the first place? How will they even know you have a mousetrap, much less a better one?

And finally, if you have <u>a better mousetrap</u> and people find out about it – what will you do with it? How can you ensure mousetrap quality control? How to become the world's best-known mousetrap? Should <u>you branch into cheese</u>? And so forth. *before you know it you making fondue & selling nachos.*

It sounds so simple. And of course, it may be simple – but that doesn't mean it's easy.

In *The Go-To Expert*, Heather Townsend and Jon Baker have produced a comprehensive, <u>practical book about how to build a client portfo-lio and/or firm *based on expertise*.</u> (Interestingly, the book itself is a marvellous example of precisely what Heather and Jon are talking about: an offering linked to a defined market, with a comprehensive package of business building tools around it.)

It may sound obvious that a professional, or a professional services firm, should build itself around an area of expertise – but it's not obvious or even necessary. Many firms, intentionally or otherwise, build their strategies around markets alone, or products alone, or based on a competitive segmentation, or a cost position, or relationships, or distribution channels. Expertise is not the only choice and it's easy to fall off track even if the choice is made.

It may also sound obvious that an expertise-based professional services firm, having chosen that as a strategy, will intuitively know just what to do – but, again, the truth is counter-intuitive. For a host of reasons – which Townsend and Baker itemise – professionals are marketing-averse, fearful of specialisation and loathe to think at a meta-level about content. Again, it's easy to fall off the track.

Whether you're a solo practitioner, interim, freelancer, salesperson or a professional services firm of any size, the ideas in this book are insightful, provocative and powerful. But it's not just an idea's book. Townsend and Baker have included a rich vein of examples, exercises, practical advice and tips, and an accompanying online Workbook. If you have trouble implementing the ideas in this book, it won't be for lack of a concrete roadmap!

And if you do implement them, you can look forward to higher levels of brand awareness, profitability, effectiveness, reputation, sales and probably personal satisfaction as well. Being a Go-To Expert is simple and not easy – but well worth the effort.

Charles H. Green, co-author of *The Trusted Advisor*,
and author of *Trust-Based Selling*
West Orange, New Jersey

Introduction

Why become the Go-To Expert?

Differentiating yourself from your peers, internally and externally, is the challenge that every professional faces. With today's clients more inclined to look for a better service or deal, the pressure is on for every firm and professional to justify their fee levels and increase the value they bring to clients. One way of curing these commercial headaches is to grow a reputation as the Go-To Expert within your marketplace and firm.

Becoming the Go-To Expert conveys kudos and status. When you achieve the status of Go-To Expert, you have the luxury of clients coming to you and being able to pick and choose those you want to work with, whilst being able to charge premium rates for your services. Which professional doesn't want this?

With job security no longer a given, senior professionals are often moving between periods of employment, freelancing and interim work. Whether you acknowledge it or not, today's senior professionals need to be able to sell themselves – not just to their current clients or current employers but also future clients and employers. This book will show you how to sell yourself in a way that feels comfortable and authentic. Regardless of your current employment status, it will show you how to build up your credibility, profile and reputation so that you are in control of your career, always in demand and never short of work again.

When you have built a reputation as the Go-To Expert it allows you to spend less time on business development – after all, your reputation and profile in the marketplace and your firm are enough to generate enquiries on their own. From our research, the single biggest challenge professionals have with business development is making the time to do it properly. This book shows you how to spend less overall time on business development, but win more profitable clients who will work with you for longer.

What makes a Go-To Expert?

A Go-To Expert can mean many things to many different people. For example, you can become a Go-To Expert in a firm by having a specialist skill set that is in demand. This specialist skill set could be as simple as 'the person who really knows their way around the IT system'. We asked people we trust for their views of what makes a Go-To Expert.

THE MARKETER'S VIEW

"A Go-To Expert must have some definable expertise, plus visibility and influence within their target market."

LEE FREDERIKSEN, MANAGING PARTNER, HINGE, AND CO-AUTHOR OF
PROFESSIONAL SERVICES MARKETING

THE JOURNALIST'S VIEW

"A Go-To Expert is someone who is authoritative. This is because they will have built up a profile in an industry or they have the ability to influence the marketplace due to their job role or profile."

GAVIN HINKS, FREELANCE JOURNALIST

THE MEDIA EXPERT'S VIEW

"There are so very many self-proclaimed experts these days. People who say 'I'm the world's top expert' or 'A thought leader in...'. Therefore, in my opinion, a true Go-To Expert will be seen by others as the Go-To Expert due to their body of work and the results they have achieved."

ALAN STEVENS, AUTHOR OF *PING, THE POCKET MEDIA COACH* AND
CO-AUTHOR OF *MEDIA MASTERS*

In this book we will help you to become a Go-To Expert by giving you tools to grow your reputation, profile and influence in order to make it easy for you to sell and market yourself.

Social media: the game changer

"The internet and social media are going to be the biggest change to professional services since they became deregulated and were allowed to advertise in the 1970s and 1980s."

LEE FREDERIKSEN, MANAGING PARTNER, HINGE, AND CO-AUTHOR OF
PROFESSIONAL SERVICES MARKETING

Five years ago, social media was very much in its infancy. The online world was still a very junior and poor relation to the face-to-face world. To gain the status of the Go-To Expert typically meant you were reliant on gatekeepers to your target audience such as journalists, editors, publishers and event organisers. However, that is not the case today. With the advent of broadband and social media, you can grow your reputation without having to go via these traditional gatekeepers.

Trust has always been important in the selling process – particularly for professional services. After all, you don't buy a big-ticket item from someone you don't trust. Historically, the trust between buyer and seller has been developed through personal contact. After all, the larger the risk the more likely a buyer will want to see the 'whites of the eyes' of the seller before they will commit to a purchase. The internet has opened up another avenue to developing trust between a buyer and seller. It is possible to develop trust in a person through reading and digesting their content over time, and beginning to trust their advice and their judgment before you meet them. Consequently, those professionals who commit to regularly producing content for their target market are more likely to get called than those who rely solely on personal contact to build trust.

The internet has largely removed the geographical barriers to professionals winning business. It has also given people access to huge amounts of knowledge. In fact, in the last two years we have produced more data than we did in all the years leading up to this point. Consequently, we are all becoming conditioned to expect that we can have access via the internet to anything, anywhere. This means that people when they want help are much more inclined to find the expert; the person who's done exactly what they are looking for, who has the specific expertise.

Typically, prospects and intermediaries will now meet you first in the online world. What do you do when you want to find an answer to a problem or issue you are facing? Google it. What do you do before you meet someone for the first time? Google their name. Only if your prospects like the look of what you do, and how you do it online, will you receive a call or email. If they don't – you will never know. Consequently, the skill of being able to build up a strong and credible reputation online is essential for every professional. This book shows you how to do this, plus how to communicate your brand and story in a compelling and credible way to your ideal clients.

Why do professionals struggle to market and sell themselves?

If you went into any service provider, such as an accountant's or doctor's practice, and asked the question, 'How many of you went into your profession in order to sell and market yourself?', I doubt you would get a single affirmative answer. This is because most professionals chose their profession because they were attracted to the technical work, not the marketing and selling side of being in the profession.

Many professionals struggle to translate their technical expertise into something that is easily understandable to the lay person. It's very easy to write more and more technically orientated copy, rather than simple, easy-to-understand material that their target audience can relate to. Consequently, as a result, they often fail to connect with their audience via their marketing efforts.

Very often the barrier that many professionals face with their marketing is a self-limiting belief that they can't openly share their thinking on a matter, i.e. 'If I share how I do something, or share our secrets, what will my clients need me for – and wouldn't our competitors nick our thinking?' These are typically just beliefs, and often not founded on anything tangible. After all, if all your expertise is something that you can share on a blog post, then it's not much expertise! Most people, even if you give them step-by-step instructions on how to do something in a blog post, will rarely execute them in the most time-effective way. After all, reading a blog can't deliver the level of expertise, insight and ability that your qualifications and number of years in the profession have given you.

Culturally, here in the UK, less so in other parts of the world, it's not the done thing to brag about your expertise or 'blow your own trumpet'. Many professionals subscribe to the view, which isn't always correct, that you should let your results do the talking for you. If professionals are to get better at marketing and selling themselves, they will need to become more comfortable with proactively saying, 'This is what I can do.'

Very often professionals are poor at marketing and selling themselves because they haven't been taught how to. All too frequently firms focus their fee earners' development on technical skills, at the expense of softer skills. Often, as a result of this focus on technical skills, and a firm's business model, there becomes an implied or even explicit culture in firms that client work is the number one priority for a fee earner. Consequently, business development can often be seen as something to do when you don't have any client work, something to delegate to the marketing department or something that can be left to the rainmakers.

Whatever your reason for picking up this book, we know that, if you take just a few actions or ideas away from this book, you will get better at marketing and selling yourself.

Why did we decide to write this book?

We specialise in working with professionals, from the owners of the very smallest professional practices right up to people in the largest and global firms. Jon tends to work mostly with partners in firms with fewer than five partners, whereas, Heather is very often working with aspiring, junior and established partners from the mid-tier and large firms who have a strong desire to build up a partner-sized portfolio. What we noticed with these two different populations of professionals was a strong desire to become the Go-To Expert within their firm and marketplace, as well as a reluctance to get out there and market and sell themselves. We found that when our clients focused and achieved this status of the Go-To Expert they found that clients came to them, rather than the other way around, and they achieved significantly better results than we – and they – expected. Not only did it help them easily attract the right type of clients, but it put them firmly back in control of their career and practice.

"Establishing your reputation is something that every professional needs to do, regardless of the stage of your career."

TIM LUSCOMBE, PRINCIPAL, KLO PARTNERS

As a result, we studied what the most successful of our clients were doing and found that we could replicate their techniques, not only for our own business but also our other client's businesses. This book is the result of us capturing what many of our very successful clients were doing naturally and turning this into a practical guide that you can use to replicate their success.

Case study 1
John Cassidy, The Headshot Guy

John has run his own photography business for many years. When the newspaper business severely cut back its usage of freelance photographers and his regular freelance work with *The Times* came to an end, he realised he had to find a new niche for himself. He knew he didn't want to get involved in the social side of photography and so, initially, started to focus on old-style corporate and PR photography.

Over time he noticed that an upsurge in people's usage of social media sites, combined with more people going into business for themselves, was resulting in a high level of demand for headshots. In 2010, he committed to his niche of headshots, raised his prices and rebranded his business and service offering to John Cassidy Headshots. It was at a business networking event where the name 'The Headshot Guy' came about, and it has stuck.

▶

John markets his business via social media, blogging, a regular newsletter, networking and speaking at events. Before he meets with prospects he sends them out a tips booklet to help them get the best headshot on the day. This helps to establish his credibility and expertise before potential clients meet him in person. John has carefully crafted his website so that any potential client can clearly see how John works and the stages in the process to help get the best headshot possible.

Over time John has honed and refined his service, offering different packages and services for six different potential markets, e.g. speakers, authors and trainers, company teams, event headshots, female entrepreneurs and business professionals. Unlike most photographers, John has thought of everything to help you get the best headshot possible, in order to communicate your personal brand. For example, he can provide a hairdresser and make-up artist, helps clients with their visual branding messages and advises on the best colours and clothing styles to wear.

As a result of building his reputation as 'The Headshot Guy', John generates all of his business by referral. As he says, to be known as the Go-To Expert by your peers and business colleagues is the perfect marketing goal. His business has grown steadily since 2010 and, in the last seven months, his reputation and profile have passed a tipping point, which has allowed him to quadruple his revenue.

Who is this book for?

This book is written for technical specialists. People such as lawyers, accountants, consultants, financial advisers, trainers, engineers, surveyors, architects, software developers, freelancers and coaches. If this is you, you know that you have time pressures and business/career goals to hit. Many of these goals probably require that you need to market and sell yourself – but selling and marketing yourself probably weren't taught to you at university or during the early stages of your career. There are many routes you can take to help you gener-ate a reputation in your marketplace as the Go-To Expert, helping you attract higher-paying and better clients by doing what you love. This book brings together all the options into once place and allows you, the reader, to choose the right path and tools for you.

This book shows you how to:

- choose, capitalise and leverage your chosen niche
- sell yourself without it feeling as if you are selling at all
- present yourself and your ideas in the best possible ways
- put firm foundations into the growth plans for your part of the business
- build a compelling proposition to attract the right type of clients
- communicate your brand externally and effectively both through face-to-face and online media
- keep your knowledge and offering fresh, regardless of the length of time you have spent in the marketplace
- build your profile by using all the different tools available, e.g. networking, writing a book/blog, public speaking, seminars and PR
- confidently convert an opportunity, when it presents itself, into real business
- manage your sales pipeline so effectively, such that you spend time only on the business worth winning
- build a team around you to be able to keep and effectively service your clients' businesses
- bring together everything you have learnt in the book, apply it to your situation and implement a plan to help you become the Go-To Expert.

If you are working within a professional practice, whether as a partner or employee, this book will:

- put you back in control of your career by giving you an easy way to build your own highly loyal client following
- help you get promoted to partner, or the next stage of partnership, because you have built your own client portfolio, which has increased the size of the partnership 'pie'

- allow you to enjoy the rewards of partnership by having a large and profitable client portfolio
- show you how to develop yourself into a thought-leader in your industry and your network, and earn status and respect for your efforts
- show you how to become one of the rainmakers in your firm.

If you have business development responsibilities for your organisation, this book will:

- show you how to build your profile and visibility to generate more leads from the right type of clients
- help you to use your profile to get introductions to prospects
- allow you to turn your networking into a well-oiled marketing machine.

If you are a self-employed technical specialist, this book will:

- show you how to spend less time on business development, because clients will be attracted to you based on your reputation and visibility
- enable you to pick and choose the right type of clients that you want to work with
- minimise the amount of time you waste with your business development because of slow-converting clients or the wrong clients wanting to work with you
- help you build a team around you to support you to achieve your career or business aims
- show you how to develop yourself into a thought-leader in your industry and your network and earn status and respect for your efforts.

If you are a partner or marketing specialist responsible for business development in your firm, it will:

- provide you with an overview of how you should help your fee earners structure and spend their business development effort
- enable you to build a reputation for your firm as thought-leaders

- minimise the amount of time and money you need to spend as a firm on business development
- show you how to use social media to help your fee earners quickly build their profile and reputation
- give you strategies and frameworks to harness the power of inbound and word-of-mouth marketing.

This book will give you the confidence, motivation, inspiration and all the information you will need to build a successful, profitable and successful practice off the back of becoming known as the Go-To Expert.

Case study 2
Carl Reader

Carl, by his own admission, fell into accountancy – more by luck than judgement. Early into his career with Dennis & Turnbull, he was given the opportunity to look after a portfolio of approximately 30 martial arts schools. He took this opportunity and got to know the key players in the industry, adjusted their services to meet the needs of the industry and, through that, learnt how to crack into a very niche industry.

Through his profile in the martial arts industry and relationships with the collection agencies that collect the fees from the schools' owners, Carl has been able to grow his portfolio of martial arts clubs and schools to 250.

His expertise in servicing martial arts clubs and schools led him to his next niche – franchising. As a result of helping one of their martial arts clients franchise his business, he gained an expertise in franchising. To help his client franchise his business, he attended a franchising exhibition in 2004. At this exhibition Carl realised that accountants either specialised in helping franchisors *or* franchisees. No one in accountancy had

▶

yet looked at the franchising marketplace holistically and how they could add value to the franchisor and franchisee by servicing both of them.

Carl used his first big franchising client win, Stagecoach Theatre Arts, to prove his credibility in the franchising marketplace. After winning Stagecoach, Carl attended as many franchising events as possible, did talks on franchising and built relationships with franchising consultants and bankers specialising in franchising. When they discovered that their conversion rate for new franchising and martial arts schools was nearly 100 per cent compared with a 33 per cent conversion rate for local business, they stopped actively marketing to local businesses. Dennis & Turnbull finds that every new client who comes from the franchising or martial arts school marketplace tends to have arrived pre-sold on the basis of at least two recommendations.

How to use this book

This book is best read through from the start to the end, then dipped in and out of as you build your own client following and practice. If this book is going to help you build a reputation as the Go-To Expert, don't ignore the exercises or questions it poses. Be brave, make a positive commitment now to your career and business by making the time to answer the questions and complete the action points and exercises in each chapter. Some of the techniques and processes will appeal to you more than others; however, we would encourage you to be curious, to keep an open mind and to have a go at using them. Some may not work for you but, until you have a go, you won't know.

At the end of each chapter are:

- exercises for you to do to put into practice what you have just learnt
- links and references to further resources.

The book is split into five parts, supported by a Workbook that you can download from **www.joinedupnetworking.com/ the-go-to-expert-workbook**

THE WORKBOOK
We want to make sure you get the most out of this book and take action, so have put together a free accompanying Workbook. Within the Workbook is a series of exercises that have been fully road-tested by our clients over the last few years. These exercises will help you get to grips with the ideas and frameworks contained in this book.

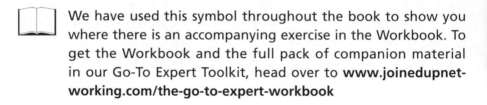 We have used this symbol throughout the book to show you where there is an accompanying exercise in the Workbook. To get the Workbook and the full pack of companion material in our Go-To Expert Toolkit, head over to **www.joinedupnet-working.com/the-go-to-expert-workbook**

Finally. . . you don't need to complete this journey alone. Both of us have played a significant part in many hundreds of professionals enjoying the rewards that come from being the Go-To Expert. We know that you can also accomplish this for yourself. Good luck on your journey and remember that we'd love to hear from you and be a real part of your support team.

Heather Townsend
heather@excedia.co.uk
Twitter:@heathertowns
LinkedIn: **www.linkedin.com/in/heathertownsend**

Jon Baker
jon@excedia.co.uk
Twitter:@divingjon
LinkedIn: **www.linkedin.com/in/jonbaker/sv**

Determining what your thing is

Regardless of what the mainstream media would like to tell you, becoming the Go-To Expert is not something that happens overnight. Building your profile and reputation takes discipline, hard work and focus. This part of the book helps you understand your motivators for becoming the Go-To Expert. After you have identified the 'why' for becoming the Go-To Expert, the book then gives you tools and techniques to enable you to actually choose what area you will become the Go-To Expert in.

1

Why do you want to become the Go-To Expert?

Topics covered in this chapter.

- What are your reasons for wanting to become the Go-To Expert?
- The importance of setting goals.
- Getting started on your journey to becoming the Go-To Expert.

To become the Go-To Expert, you need to be passionate about what you do and why you do it. This strong passion is going to be the reason why you:

- get up stupidly early to go out to meet a client on a cold, wet winter morning
- face and overcome your personal demons
- successfully sell what you do to others just by your enthusiasm for what you do and how you do it
- pick yourself up after every knock-back.

In this chapter, you will be challenged to identify why it's important for you and your future to become the Go-To Expert. You will use the downloadable Go-To Expert Workbook as you work through this book.

"The most important ingredient of being successful is to know and be able to articulate to everyone what you want from your business, your career and your life."

SIMON CHAPLIN, OWNER OF PULL YOUR SOCKS UP SIMON AND
AUTHOR OF *7 SAVVY STORIES*

What are your reasons for wanting to become the Go-To Expert?

There was a reason why you picked up this book. At this point in time, that reason may be buried in your subconscious. It's now time to dig it out from your subconscious and get clarity on why it's so important for you to become the Go-To Expert. To find this clarity, you may find it helpful to ask yourself a series of 'Why?' questions.

> **1st question** *Why is becoming the Go-To Expert important to me?*
>
> **2nd question** *Why is the answer to the 1st question important to me?*
>
> **3rd question** *Why is the answer to the 2nd question important to me?*

. . . and so on.

Continue asking yourself these questions until you reach one of two answers like these:

- 'Just because.'
- 'Well, it's not really important to me.'

When you have reached the *Just because* answer, normally you will have uncovered a key driver or motivator for you. If you reach the *Well, it's not really important to me*, it's very likely that you've identified a reason that your family, friends or others have given to you.

A real-life example will illustrate this questioning process.

> Raj wanted to become the Go-To Expert for wills and probate for small business owners. He asked himself a series of 'Why?' questions
>
> **Question** *Why is it important for me to become the Go-To Expert for small business owners for wills and probate?*
>
> I need to differentiate myself from the other private client solicitors in my firm (and other local firms).

Question *Why do I need to differentiate myself from the other private client solicitors in my firm?*

So that I can start to build my own client portfolio and become easier for others to refer to.

Question *Why do I want my own client portfolio?*

So that I can get promoted to partner or start my own practice.

Question *Why do I want to get promoted to partner or start my own practice?*

Because I like the status that comes with being a partner or running my own practice – and hopefully the financial rewards as well.

Question *Why do I want the status and financial rewards?*

Just because. . .

As a result of asking himself these questions, Raj decided to build his reputation as the Go-To Expert for wills and probate for small businesses as he believed that this would be an important part of his strategy to get to partner.

Reason why exercise

For you, does becoming the Go-To Expert mean any of the following?

- Being head-hunted for your next job?
- Being known in your firm as the person to go to for 'x'?
- Having a client portfolio containing the types of clients you want to work for?
- Being paid for doing what you love?
- Regularly getting your articles published by magazines and newspapers?
- Being a destination point for journalists who want quotes or content for their articles?
- Getting regularly asked to speak at events and conferences?

- Being able to charge a certain level of fees for your services?
- Something else?

Once you know what becoming the Go-To Expert means for you, then you can set meaningful and measurable goals to achieve this.

Case study 1
Caitlyn

Caitlyn was an interim recruiter in a traditionally run recruitment consultancy. She believed that she needed to change the way she won business, i.e. via a large focus on outbound calls, if she was ever going to be the top consultant on the team. She looked at her list of clients and successfully placed candidates and noticed that she was having a reasonable amount of success in placing marketing specialists. As a result, she decided to become known for placing marketing interims. She set herself a goal to triple the size of her network of senior interim marketing specialists. After 12 months of focusing on building up these relationships, and regularly writing articles for senior interim marketing specialists looking for roles, her strategy started to pay dividends. She found that at least 30 per cent of all her new business came to her via her network rather than relying on outbound calls. Within 18 months, she was promoted twice due to her success in winning business.

The importance of setting goals

Athletes, and other successful people who are driving themselves forward for success, use goal-setting to establish a future focus, then the milestones along the way give them short-term motivation. Having clarity on goals allows you to decide whether something is or is not a priority, i.e. do you need to invest time in this?

Goal-setting will focus your acquisition of knowledge and help you to organise your time and resources so that you can make the most of the opportunities that come your way. By setting sharp, clearly defined goals, you can measure your achievements of those goals and you will make progress in what previously may have felt like a long pointless grind. Your self-confidence will also improve as you achieve your goals.

Some professionals worry about whether people around them, including clients, will see them as 'pushy' if they set goals and are open about their career and business aspirations. Actually, telling other people about your goals is an excellent way of committing yourself to action.

The differences between goals, milestones and objectives

Goals: These are what you want to achieve in the future. They can be measured in some way.

Milestones: These are sub-goals, which, if achieved, will help you realise your goals. Like your goals, these can be measured in some way.

Objectives: These are the specific, measurable actions you will do to accomplish your milestones.

Examples

Goal: To become the Go-To Expert for tax for technology businesses within five years.

Milestones

- I will be asked to join the firm's technology sector team within two years.
- Within 12 months, I will have 3 technology clients within my portfolio.
- Within 18 months I will have an article published in the *Engineering and Technology Magazine*.

▶

Objectives

● Every month, brainstorm ideas for articles to pitch to the technology press.

● Gain agreement from the head of the firm's technology sector team that he/she will be my mentor, by January.

● Identify all the partners who specialise in working with technology businesses and set up a conversation with them to understand the challenges these businesses face, by April.

Getting started on your journey to becoming the Go-To Expert

"The journey of a thousand miles starts with one single step."

LAO TZU, CHINESE PHILOSOPHER

Don't confuse good intentions with action. Sometimes we find that professionals delay committing to a specialism until they have reached a certain point in their career or with their business, e.g., 'After I have got this many clients I can then afford to specialise', 'When I move to my next firm I can specialise...' There will never be a right time to get started, but, if you are serious about becoming the Go-To Expert, the time to take action is now. Merely saying you want something won't make it happen!

"The road to hell is paved with good intentions."

ENGLISH PROVERB

It's time to identify your goals to help you become the Go-To Expert. To help crystallise these, it's often helpful to imagine you are taking a video of that moment in time when you have achieved your goals. What can you see? What can you hear? What will you have achieved? Using this picture in your mind, now write down your goals. For example, one of our clients, Janet, wanted to become the change management guru for public-sector bodies. She initially told us what it meant for her:

"I know I will have got there when I find that I am asked to speak at industry conferences and have an income that is higher than when I was employed. I will not be worried about the phone ringing any more and probably will have employed another pair of hands to cope with the demand for my services."

We challenged her to make this picture of the future more tangible, i.e. turn these indicators into measurable goals.

This is what she said.

- More than 80 per cent of my business will be helping public-sector bodies successfully manage large-scale change projects, typically involving the introduction of new technology.
- I will generate more than £20,000 fees per month and employ a project manager within my team.
- All my business will come to me from repeat business, referrals from my existing clients or people who have read my blog or heard me speak.
- My marketing and sales processes and systems will work effectively so I hit my revenue target of £20,000+ a month.
- I will speak at four major public-sector conferences a year.

 **Goal-setting exercise**

Summary

Before you can start working towards becoming the Go-To Expert you need to understand your personal motivation for doing so. Once you understand your reason why you can then define what being the Go-To Expert actually means for you. This definition then forms the basis of your goals within your Go-To Expert Plan.

Action points

1 Ask professionals you consider to be Go-To Experts how they have built up their profile and visibility. Listen to what they say and adopt one tip or tactic they have used and apply this to your own situation.

2 Put a task in your diary to revisit your definition of the Go-To Expert every three months. Is it still what you want and valid for you and your situation?

Further resources

For help to think through what you want to achieve in your career, we recommend these resources.

BOOKS

- Townsend, H. and Larbie, J. (2012) *How to Make Partner and Still Have a Life*, London: Kogan Page
- Maun, R. (2012) *Bouncing Back: How to get going again after a career setback*, Singapore: Marshall Cavendish Business

WEBSITES

- Richard Maun's blog: **www.richardmaun.com/writing**
- How to make partner and still have a life: **www.howtomakepartner.com**

2

What is going to be your thing?

Topics covered in this chapter.

- What do we mean by a niche?
- The importance of being committed to your niche.
- Why professionals resist adopting a niche.
- How to find your niche.
- What research you need to do to get underneath the skin of your niche.
- Deciding on your niche.

"The expectation that you can now find a top expert, who will be accessible to you, has led to the recent rise in specialisation. This has given firms or individuals who have a well-defined or specific expertise a big commercial advantage."

LEE FREDERIKSEN, MANAGING PARTNER, HINGE, AND CO-AUTHOR OF
PROFESSIONAL SERVICES MARKETING

You've picked up this book because you want to be seen as the Go-To Expert. Therefore, what do you want to be known as the Go-To Expert for? On the surface of it, a very simple question, but very often a tough question to answer. This chapter will help you answer that question by helping you take the first step in the process to becoming the Go-To Expert: deciding on your niche.

This chapter will help you understand the commercial and personal reasons why you need to find and decide on your niche. Your future success as the Go-To Expert depends on how committed you are to your niche.

What do we mean by a niche?

"We shouldn't kid ourselves that we are experts at everything because we are not. The reason we become so successful when we specialise in a niche is because we have expertise in a tightly defined area. By becoming an expert to a niche we become more important and valuable to our clients in the niche."

ALAN STEVENS, AUTHOR OF *PING, THE POCKET MEDIA COACH* AND
CO-AUTHOR OF *MEDIA MASTERS*

Everybody keeps talking about 'having a niche', but what is this 'niche' thing – and should you be worried if you don't have one?

The dictionary defines your niche as:

- a situation or activity specially suited to a person's interests, abilities or nature
- relating to or aimed at a small specialised group or market.

When we talk about your niche in this book, we are referring to these definitions of a niche, i.e. where your particular passion and technical talents are used to cater for one particular specialist audience. Without a niche, clients will see you as identical to your peers. When you establish a niche of your own, it allows you to specialise and become the Go-To Expert on your chosen topic.

Let's take some examples of where professionals have used their niches to become Go-To Experts.

- Tim Luscombe who is known as the corporate finance speaker.
- Alan Stevens who helps people protect and manage their reputation.
- David Kaye who is known as the legal expert for entrepreneurial retail businesses.

Your niche is just one part of your personal brand. However, your niche and how well you capitalise on your niche will heavily influence the rest of your personal brand, i.e.:

- how you communicate to the external world
- how you choose to dress when in 'professional' mode
- the technology you choose to adopt, e.g., are you an Apple or an Android person?

Case study 1
Leon

Leon is a business mentor who specialises in helping business owners to grow their businesses. His own business development efforts were being held back by trying to be all things to all businesses, i.e. not having a niche. We examined his clients to see which type of clients he really enjoyed working with *and* got the best results with. As a result of doing this exercise, Leon realised he got the best results when he worked with highly technical experts, in particular IT consultancy clients. After adopting this niche, Leon's revenue doubled and the time he spent on business development reduced by a third.

Case study 2
Sammy

Sammy wanted to get promoted to director in his firm of insurance brokers. However, before he could be promoted he needed to show his partners that he was able to go out and win work. He set out to become the Go-To Expert for property companies that needed insurance. Twelve months later his hard work paid off when he built a large enough client portfolio to get promoted to director.

The importance of being committed to your niche

REASON 1: IT HELPS YOU TO BE REFERRED AND RECOMMENDED MORE OFTEN

When people buy professional services, they are generally buying a high-value product, service or person. For this reason there has to be a high degree of trust between the buyer and seller before the purchase takes place. This means that a potential buyer of professional services prefers to act on a referral or recommendation of someone they know, like and trust before engaging in a conversation with a potential supplier. If you are fortunate enough to be recommended, it means they are placing trust in you, not the company that employs you.

The recent rapid growth and adoption of social media has led to people being able to quickly generate a strong online personal brand and rapidly communicate their brand's promise via word-of-mouth referrals. Social media is also enabling people to maintain networks vastly bigger than a network based on face-to-face interactions alone. Five years ago you may have had only one or two people within your network whom you would be happy to recommend. Today, you are only one click or Google search away from generating five or six recommendations of people within your network. It's the strength and marketability of your personal brand that is the determining factor in terms of whether or not you will be the person others recommend.

REASON 2: IT HELPS YOUR MARKETING MATERIALS TO BE MORE EFFECTIVE

When you are clear about your brand, your marketing materials become more effective. This is because you know:

- where to place your marketing materials and content so that they are read by your niche
- the right buttons to press to build an emotional connection with your audience that compels them to take action quickly, e.g. contact you
- how to package up your services so that they are a good fit, solving your niche's problems.

REASON 3: IT IS FUNDAMENTAL TO YOU AND/OR YOUR FIRM'S FUTURE GROWTH

Sometimes people can feel 'stuck' or stalled, with nowhere to go in their career. Growth opportunities can come when you define your niche, since the niche leads your thinking and whole approach into areas you had never fully considered before.

REASON 4: IT ENABLES YOU TO DIFFERENTIATE YOURSELF FROM YOUR PEERS

Look at any accountant, lawyer or architect's website and you will find it will probably mention most of these words:

- proactive
- speak your language
- value for money.

When you compare one technical specialist with a competitor, it's often very difficult to differentiate them from each other. This is why you need to be niched. In the 'FT Effective Client–Adviser Relationships Report published in 2012, it found that 40 per cent of buyers of professional services have 'being a sector specialist' in their top three buying criteria, and 67 per cent of buyers want to work with an adviser who has a deep understanding of their business and marketplace.[1]

REASON 5: IT ALLOWS YOU TO TAILOR YOUR SERVICE TO WHAT YOUR CLIENTS WANT AND NEED, MAKING IT EASIER TO CONVERT PROSPECTS INTO CLIENTS

When you adopt a niche, you can tailor the services you offer very closely to your niche's needs, lifestyle and problems. Let's illustrate this with two examples: a specialist wedding photographer versus a portrait photographer who does a bit of everything. Which of these two photographers are you more likely to decide to call to help you on your wedding day?

[1] FT Effective Client–Adviser Relationships Report 2012, **www.ftcorporate.ft.com/professional-services**

MARK – PORTRAIT PHOTOGRAPHER	I do portraiture: graduation, family memories, event photography, retirement photos, your baby's first year, weddings. Call me to discuss your requirements.
TOM AND BEN – CAPTURING THE MAGIC OF YOUR WEDDING DAY	We will be by your side for every step of your special day. Our cameras will capture the essence of your wedding day, being with you from 7 a.m. to midnight. Call us to tell us how we can help you create an album of amazing memories to be enjoyed for many years to come.

REASON 6: IT HELPS YOU TO FORM STRATEGIC ALLIANCES

One of the easiest ways for any professional to win work is to form strategic alliances with other professionals offering complementary services. For example, Karen is a solicitor who specialises in wills and, when there is a complex rural property to be sold, she readily recommends her clients use Richard, a surveyor who brands himself as the 'Boots & Land Rover man'. Likewise, it is not uncommon for farmers to use Richard to discuss purchases and amalgamations of properties and Richard suggests Karen to arrange the conveyancing. In both cases, clients feel they are being handed over to a trusted friend.

REASON 7: IT ALLOWS YOU AND YOUR FIRM TO CHARGE A PREMIUM FEE FOR YOUR SERVICES

From personal experience, we can relate acutely to the pain of submitting a proposal and worrying about whether you are too expensive or too cheap. Wouldn't it be easy if there were a standard tariff that every accountant, lawyer, coach or trainer conformed to? Sadly, this will never be the case. But, what makes the difference between an accountant who can command £300+ hourly rates and one who struggles to get more than £70 hourly rates? Very often it is the perception of the value that each accountant brings to the work. If you have the profile of *the expert* in what you do, clients are often happier to pay significantly more for your services.

REASON 8: IT MINIMISES CLIENT CHURN

If your clients know and realise that you truly understand their needs and requirements – plus speak their language – they are less likely to be attracted away to one of your general competitors with a cheaper alternative solution.

Why professionals resist adopting a niche

After reading through the eight solid commercial reasons for adopting a niche, you may wonder why so many professionals resist niching themselves. There are typically three reasons why this is:

1 you think you will turn business away
2 you fear boredom dealing with only one type of client
3 you have no idea where to start.

YOU THINK YOU WILL TURN BUSINESS AWAY

As a specialist in a specific area, your marketing will be optimised to attract the right sort of clients – the ones you really want to work with and find rewarding in more than just the fiscal sense. What would you do if somebody else approached you? You would decide if you had the capacity to take them on or not. You don't have to turn them away; you just don't market to them.

Many professionals worry that if they adopt a niche then they will alienate their existing clients who don't belong within that niche. Remember that your marketing is not aimed at your existing clients, just the new ones you want to win. If you are delivering a great or even extraordinary level of service, your existing clients probably wouldn't care less about your niche. However, you may find that, to deliver the right level of service to the niche clients, you need to leave some older clients.

YOU FEAR BOREDOM DEALING WITH ONLY ONE TYPE OF CLIENT

The common arguments go like this.

- 'I like the variety that being a jack-of-all-trades brings me.'
- 'I started my firm to get a greater variety of work and enjoy myself more. If I niche I will only get one type of client and that means I won't be as happy.'
- 'If I am to get allocated to more clients at work I need a broader skill set to be more appealing to the managers and partners resourcing the client's work.'

This is a very real fear. Your long-term success depends on being clear on what you want, emotionally as much as (if not more than) financially, but then think a bit more. Variety comes from the people you have as clients, more so than the topic you have chosen as your niche.

A niche is about marketing and profile building. It's about focus and allowing you to have marketing that is very attractive, versus marketing that doesn't really speak to anybody. It's about being an obvious choice for people in that niche. That leads to you becoming the Go-To Expert for your marketplace.

Having mastered one, who's to say you don't start another one or two niches?

Case study 3
Sarah

Sarah is a financial adviser who specialises in working with lawyers. As her client base grew she found herself increasingly attracting clients who were accountants in practice who had similar problems to the lawyers she worked with. As a result, Sarah produced two sets of marketing materials, one tailored to legal clients and the other tailored to her accountancy clients.

Case study 4
Curtis

Curtis started off as his firm's expert on networking. Whenever the firm had a client who wanted to run networking training, it was Curtis who was booked for the job. As time went on and Curtis developed his skill in social networking, his firm started to market his services for social media training as well as networking training.

Early on in your professional career you do need a good spread of technical knowledge. However, as soon as you are qualified, this is when you will start to make yourself more attractive for allocating to client work by specialising.

YOU HAVE NO IDEA WHERE TO START

Understandably, it's one thing to say that you have a niche and another to actually commit to it and capitalise on your niche. Read on to the next part of this chapter to find out how to discover and decide on your niche.

How to find your niche

"People become known as the experts because they love what they do, because of how passionate they are about their subject matter and those they want to help. You can't learn that from lists, you have to feel it, to believe it."

SONJA JEFFERSON, CO-AUTHOR OF *VALUABLE CONTENT MARKETING*

The hard part of finding a niche is identifying and choosing one that you are passionate about, *confident* that there is enough of a market, it will be motivated to buy your services *and* you will make a good living from it. For example, if you are an architect, you could decide to specialise in residential eco-housing developments. This is definitely specific enough. However, would there be enough work in your practice to build up a profitable client portfolio around this niche?

You often hear people saying, 'Follow your passion and the money will follow'. We disagree with this statement. Money will follow your passion only if there is a marketplace willing to buy what you are passionate about! People often flourish when they are working in an environment, business or team that is well suited to their particular personality type.

EXAMPLES OF POOR NICHES	EXAMPLES OF GOOD NICHES
Executive coach to board directors *Isn't that what every executive coach is offering?*	Executive coach to board directors of retail companies
Commercial lawyer *There are huge numbers of commercial lawyers. What makes you different from all the others?*	Commercial lawyer specialising in working with fast-growing technology companies
Architect specialising in working with timber frame houses within urban regeneration projects *Is this the sort of specialism that this marketplace will pay for?*	Architect specialising in urban regeneration projects
Accountant specialising in owner-managed businesses (OMBs). *This is what most mid-tier and small firms of accountants specialise in*	Accountant specialising in working with owner-managed financial services businesses

To help you draw up a shortlist of potential niches that you could adopt, think about the answers to these questions.

- With what type of clients or people do you love working?
- What kinds or clients or work do you find others in your firm (or outside of your firm) recommend you for?
- What type of clients or work suit your personality?
- Where in your past career history have you thrived and why?
- In what type of environment do you thrive?

- Is there a big enough marketplace in which you can build a profitable client portfolio?
- With what audiences, technical skills or types of clients do you already have credibility working?
- In which sectors or marketplaces do you have a strong, influential and supportive network?
- In what marketplaces does the firm want to maintain or strengthen its presence?
- Which sectors have a growing demand for your technical skill set?
- Which sectors are poorly served by your competitors?

Tip

The right niche for you will be one in which you have a commercial benefit coupled with an emotional connection to the niche.

What research you need to do to get underneath the skin of your niche

To get underneath the skin of your niche market and find the potential candidates for your niche, we recommend doing research to find the answers to these questions.

- What characteristics do the players in your niche share?
- What challenges or problems do they typically face?
- What problems can I solve for them?
- Which companies/organisations or individuals do they typically work with or associate with?
- Where do they socialise online and in the 'real' world?
- Where do I already have examples of how I have helped my niche or solved problems similar to what they are experiencing?

The answers to these questions will help you truly commit to your niche by helping you adapt your service proposition to your niche's requirements, (see Chapter 3) and guide you on what to put into your content plan (see Chapter 5).

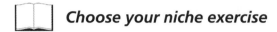 *Choose your niche exercise*

Deciding on your niche

Now you have done your research into the potential marketplace for each of your shortlisted niches, you are probably in a position to commit to niching yourself. If you can't decide between some of the potential niches you have identified, then think about which of your niches you have:

- the most passion for
- the most credibility in
- the most engaged and largest network
- more potential for strategic alliances already available to you
- the most current or ex-clients in
- the most excitement for when you think about specialising in this area.

Tip

It may seem to be ideal to be the first person to adopt a certain niche. Before you take this step, though, do check that there is a marketplace for your offering.

Summary

The first step towards becoming the Go-To Expert is to decide on your niche, i.e. the audience you will specialise in servicing with your technical skill set.

To choose your niche, consider:

- what you are already known for
- where your network is the largest and most engaged
- where you have the greatest potential for strategic alliances for the least amount of work
- where you have large clusters of current or ex-clients
- the amount of excitement you feel when you think about specialising in this area
- where your firm has identified sectors or specialist areas to invest in for future growth.

When you have chosen your niche, you need to be able to succinctly state whom you will specialise in working with and the value you will bring to them.

Remember that adopting a niche helps you acquire *new* clients. If you give your *current* clients good service, normally they will stay with you – regardless of whether they fall within your current niche or not.

Action points

1 Look around you and see what types of specialisms are common in your general field. Do check LinkedIn, your professional association/body and ask your peers. Write these down in a list and highlight any that you could see yourself doing.

2 Ask professionals you trust and admire how they chose their niche and the impact it has made on their business and career.

3 Ask your network, peers or the partners in your firm what industries, sectors or specialist skills are likely to be in demand with clients and the marketplace generally over the next five years.

4 Use the choose your niche exercise in the Go-To Expert Workbook to decide on your niche.

5 Find two online magazines or blogs in your niche area and start subscribing to them now.

Further resources

To help you find your niche and explore your personal brand in more depth, we recommend these resources.

BOOKS

- Brown, R. (2007) *How to Build Your Reputation: The secrets of becoming the 'go to' professional in a crowded marketplace*, Penryn: Ecademy Press
- Holloway, J. (2013) *Personal Branding for Brits: A practical guide to blowing your own trumpet without sounding like an eejit*, Skipton: Spark Ltd
- Purkiss, J. and Royston-Lee, D. (2012) *Brand You: Turn your talents into a winning formula*, Harlow: Pearson, 2nd edn
- Schawbel, D. (2010) *Me 2.0: 4 steps to building your future*, New York: Kaplan Trade, 2nd edn

WEBSITES

- Spark: Personal Branding for Business **www.sparkexec.co.uk**
- Personal Branding Blog **www.personalbrandingblog.com**
- How to make partner and still have a life **www.howtomakepartner.com** (do a search on niche)
- Venture-Now **www.venture-now.com** (do a search for 'niche')

Packaging your brand

If you are going to become the Go-To Expert, you need to have a strong brand in your marketplace that is instantly recognisable and easily referrable. Before you spend any time or money on marketing activities, such as networking, you must have put the time and thought into building this strong brand. For example:

- How to package your expertise so you become irresistible to potential clients.
- How to create the right first impression wherever your potential client meets you.
- The role of content in attracting and retaining clients.
- How to use a blog to build your profile and visibility.

3

How to make your services irresistible to clients

Topics covered in this chapter.

- What you need to know about your niche to build a successful marketing plan.
- Deciding what services to offer.
- How to package up your services.
- How to differentiate yourself from your colleagues and competitors in the eyes of your niche market.
- Removing the risk for your clients.

Having completed the Action Points in Part 1, you should be quite clear in which subject(s) you want to be the Go-To Expert and have worked out your underlying motivational drivers. Using those as foundations, this chapter will explore how to package your service(s) in a way that will make them irresistible to your niche market.

Regardless of whether you run your own firm or are a senior professional working in a partnership, you need to be clear about what services you offer to your clients. This chapter challenges you to think about the services you offer and how to present them to make them more enticing to your niche market.

What you need to know about your niche to build a successful marketing plan

"If you are truly going to become a Go-To Expert, you need to be aware of your client's perspective; what they are looking for, and how you can help solve their problems. The more time you spend with clients being curious about their world, not trying to sell, will repay your investment many times over."

SHIREEN SMITH, IP SOLICITOR, AZRIGHTS, AND AUTHOR OF *LEGALLY BRANDED*

The first step in building your marketing plan is to research your niche. For example, the niche market for Julie, an image consultant, is professionals who work in a partnership, such as lawyers and accountants. Whilst Julie could work with other professionals such as bankers, she has decided to narrow down her niche to lawyers and accountants as she spent ten years working for legal and accountancy firms.

 Getting to know you exercise

WAYS TO RESEARCH YOUR NICHE MARKET

- Read the trade-related press, blogs and articles.
- Follow companies and individuals from your niche market on social media, e.g. LinkedIn, Twitter, Facebook, Google+.
- Attend relevant industry events, such as conferences and seminars.
- Interview people who work within the industry, particularly your existing clients.
- Run focus groups for people within the industry or customers/clients of your niche market.
- Send out a survey or questionnaire.
- Read online forums.
- Read the websites, blogs, reports and white papers provided by your competitors.
- Sign up for newsletters from your competitors and niche market.

Deciding what services to offer

Typically, your clients will be driven to buy your services by a pain point, i.e. a deep-seated emotional, rather than logical, reason. This may seem counter-intuitive at first so let us explain. The initial impulse to hire you is always an emotional one, then backed up by logical and rational reasons to buy your services. Your research will help you to really drill down into these pain points, which will be the underlying reasons why your niche market will want to buy your services. These pain points will form the basis of the services you offer to your clients. The five whys and pain points exercises in the Workbook will help you work out the real pain points that will motivate your niche market to buy from you.

The five whys exercise

Pain points exercise

Your sound bite

So, now you have identified your pain points and completed the five whys exercise, you need to have something that helps you communicate this. We call this a sound bite and it helps you anchor who you help and the results you help them to achieve. To build your sound bite, fill in the blanks below.

- Who I help: ....
- The pain points they face are: ....
- The outcomes my solution achieves are: ....

Then craft your answer into a single sentence.

Sound bite exercise

EXAMPLES OF GOOD SOUND BITES

Gary, presentation skills trainer '*I help salespeople win more work by becoming accomplished and confident presenters.*'

Julie, image consultant '*I help female lawyers and accountants feel confident at work when returning after maternity leave.*'

Shirley, tax accountant '*I help retailers to maximise their profits by paying the least amount of tax.*'

Brian, intellectual property lawyer '*I help technology companies protect their business's assets and gain an advantage over their competitors by helping them trademark and patent their intellectual property.*'

How to package up your services

As the services that professionals offer are generally considered purchases – they involve a high level of reputational or financial risk – most potential clients are not willing to jeopardise either their money or reputation by opting for your most expensive service offering first. They will want to trial your services in a small, preferably risk-free, way. As a result, you need to be able to provide different services at different price points to suit your niche market's particular challenges, preferences and budgets. Use the product ladder exercise in the Workbook to help you think through the different types of services you will offer.

 Product ladder exercise

TARGET CLIENT (AND NEED YOU ARE SOLVING FOR THEM)	PRODUCTS AND SERVICES			
	FREE	**LOW COST**	**BUDGET**	**CHAMPAGNE**
Individual wealth-maximising service	Guide to tax planning for solicitor practices	Wealth check R&D tax credit check	Partner's tax return Financial planning service	Aggressive tax-planning schemes for the practice
Succession planning service			Individual exit planning sessions Succession planning annual meeting	
Compliance			Annual accounts filed and audited Corporation tax return	
New partner's equity planning service				Firm valuations and capital entry requirements

Figure 3.1 Example of a product ladder

Case study 1
GreenStones

When Simon Chaplin bought his firm it was a fairly typical independent accountancy practice in Peterborough doing compliance work and giving a little bit of business advice. Simon wanted to make his firm dramatically different and really stand out in his local marketplace. He implemented a raft of very successful initiatives, but one of the most successful ones was changing the service to become more clientcentric by offering fixed fees. At the time, this was almost unheard of. Whenever Simon went to a networking event and talked about how the practice was different from other firms and offered fixed fees, he was always inundated with enquiries from people there. This demand for the firm's services allowed the firm to increase its fees by 30 per cent within 18 months of changing how it charged its clients. Within three years of Simon owning the firm, driven by the strategy of becoming clientcentric and dramatically different, it doubled its headcount, tripled its revenue and quadrupled its profits.

Case study 2
David Kaye

In 1985 David set up his own legal practice in Scotland. His big break came in 1989 when he started working with a discount retailer, What Everyone Wants, which at the time was a household name in Scotland. David was invited on to its board, on a retainer basis, as its legal director and company secretary. As a result of doing this, David realised that there were many other similar-sized organisations that wanted the ease of being able to speak to a trusted legal adviser, who really understood their businesses, without worrying about the clock ticking and being billed for every phone call or meeting. From this point onwards, David's main service to his clients was this 'outsourced legal department'. David has found, by adopting this business model, that he can be truly integrated into his clients' businesses, as a quasi non-executive director, and give them far more valuable legal advice. Adopting this non-traditional business model has been one of the major causes of David's successful career as a business lawyer.

How to differentiate yourself from your colleagues and competitors in the eyes of your niche market

If a potential client asked you today why they should buy your services rather than those of one of your peers or someone from another firm, could you answer this question succinctly? At this stage we are not talking about you having a unique selling proposition (USP), just some clear statements as to why your potential clients would choose to work with *you*.

Case study 3
Joseph Frasier Solicitors

Joseph Frasier Solicitors specialises in working with deaf and hard-of-hearing clients. Such people find it very difficult to work with solicitors, as most solicitors require a face-to-face conversation or phone-based communication. So, Joseph Frasier has tailored its services to this market by:

▶

- training all its staff in sign language
- providing the option for clients to talk to their solicitors by Skype rather than having to use the phone
- specialising in industrial deafness personal injury claims.

Very often it is not the services you offer, but *how* you deliver those services that will help you to differentiate yourself. After all, for most professionals it is very hard to differentiate themselves based on the services they offer. For example, one conveyancer normally offers a very similar service to another conveyancer. Like Joseph Frasier, you need to be able to articulate 'why you' in your marketing messages. Use the why you exercise in the Workbook to help you think through what features, and how they are delivered, you want to offer to your clients.

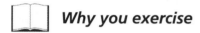 *Why you exercise*

Removing the risk for your clients

Buying professional services always involves a risk for the buyer. This may be a reputational or financial risk. For example, Steven, a business coach, realised that many business owners don't buy the services of a business coach because they are concerned that the business coach may not be able to help them achieve their goals. As a result, Steven always offers a guarantee to his clients that, if he doesn't help them achieve their goals, and they do their next steps from the sessions, he will refund their fees.

What features can you add in to your service offering to either remove this risk or reduce it?

- A guarantee?
- A no win, no fee arrangement?
- A refund?
- An insurance policy?

For example, Gary, a presentation skills trainer, who specialises in helping salespeople sell more by becoming confident and accomplished presenters, added in a guarantee for every delegate who booked on his 'Perfect pitch' and 'Presenting for nervous wrecks' workshops. His guarantee stated that, if his delegates completed their post-course action plan and didn't increase their conversion rate with new clients by 10 per cent within 12 months of attending the workshop, he would refund their course fees.

Summary

The services that you offer are designed to help your niche market eliminate a pain point. The deeper and more emotive the pain point, the stronger the likelihood that your niche market will take action and buy from you. By being innovative about the features you offer within your services, you will be able to differentiate yourself from your competitors and become irresistible to your clients.

Action points

1 Write out your sound bite and test it on trusted colleagues. Listen to their feedback and alter your sound bite to improve it.

2 When you next attend a networking event, listen out for people's sound bites. Which ones resonate for you and why? What can you learn from them? Try your sound bite out, too.

3 Read your competitors' websites and marketing material. How are they differentiating themselves? How do they reduce the risk for new clients buying from them? What can you adapt from their service offerings to make your offerings more attractive to your niche market?

4 Talk through your proposed services and sound bite with your niche market. Ask for their feedback and check that you have identified their pain points correctly. Make adjustments to your sound bite as necessary.

Further resources

For help to think through what you services you want to offer your clients, and how to package them up, we recommend these resources.

BOOKS

- Schultz, M., Doerr, J. E., Frederiksen, L. (2013) *Professional Services Marketing: How the best firms build premier brands, thriving lead generation engines, and cultures of business development success*, Hoboken, NJ: John Wiley & Sons
- Thomas, B. (2013) *Watertight Marketing: Delivering long-term sales results*, St Albans: Anoma Press
- Townsend, H. and Larbie, J. (2012) *How to Make Partner and Still Have a Life*, London: Kogan Page, Ch. 17 and 18

WEBSITES

- *Watertight Marketing* **www.watertightmarketing.com**
- Hinge Marketing **www.hingemarketing.com**

4

How to craft the right impression

Topics covered in this chapter.

- Your personal marketing toolkit.
- How to dress the part.
- Social media etiquette.

"Almost everyone will make a good first impression, but only a few will make a good lasting impression."

SONYA PARKER

Your personal marketing toolkit

Your personal marketing toolkit will include everything you, as the Go-To Expert, will require to attract new clients. Depending on your personal circumstances, it will include some or all of the following:

- credibility statements
- credibility stories
- relationship hooks
- website
- blog
- business card
- biographies, including your author credit, short bio and long bio
- one-page credentials document about you or your firm
- professional photos, including a head and shoulders shot
- speaker kit, including show reel, one-pager about you and what you speak about, introduction to you to be read out at events where you are speaking (see Chapter 8)
- social media profiles – LinkedIn, Twitter, Facebook, Google+

- name badge
- templates for slides, documents and handouts
- press kit
- series of two–three-minute video clips of you presenting, being interviewed, talking to camera
- client list, testimonials and case studies.

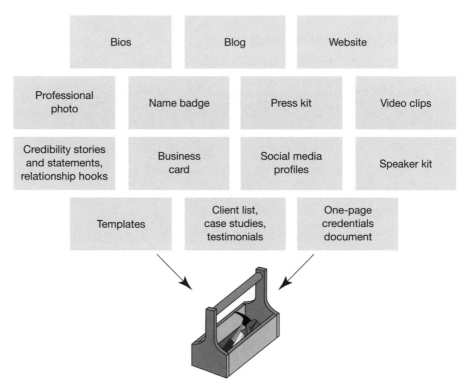

Figure 4.1 The contents of your personal marketing kit

CREDIBILITY STATEMENTS AND STORIES

As the saying goes, your reputation precedes you. However, you can actively help people to quickly grasp what you are the Go-To Expert for by means of the statement and stories you use. These are what we call credibility statements and stories. Much of your personal marketing toolkit will be based on these.

Identifying your credibility statements

Credibility statements demonstrate, in some way, your status as the Go-To Expert. These could be:

- the length of time you have practised
- the professional qualifications you hold
- awards, honours, prizes and professional recognition you have received for your expertise
- who you have worked for
- what other people have said about you, particularly influential people in your industry
- the books and articles you have written
- your job title, particularly if you are a partner, managing partner or head of a sector team
- the conferences at which you have spoken
- when you have featured in the media, e.g. radio or TV appearances, quotes in the national, trade or local press.

Tip

The best credibility statements are the ones where you have been invited to do something as a result of the profile and reputation you have generated. For example:

'I have been invited twice to present at the Chartered Institute of Personnel and Development's annual conference.'

Your credibility statements typically are easily memorable, repeatable and normally short statements that allow anyone talking about you to instantly convey your credibility. For example, one of our clients is a video and TV broadcast expert. When we recommend him to anyone, we always mention that he has spent 30 years working for the BBC and taught a well-known UK TV personality how to present. These two short credibility statements consistently establish his competence and reputation as a technical expert.

Credibility statements exercise

Here are some real examples of credibility statements used by Go-To Experts in their LinkedIn profiles.

Charles Green: 'When it comes to Trusted Advisor, I wrote the book – literally.'

Ian Brodie: 'I was recently named as one of the "Top 50 Global Thought Leaders in Marketing and Sales" by *Top Sales World* magazine, and one of the "Top 25 Global Influencers in Sales and Sales and Sales Management" by OpenView Labs.'

Credibility stories illustrate what you do, who you do it for and the results that you help your clients achieve. They are succinct and, unlike most stories, have no middle. You may have heard them being called war stories or sales stories.

A typical credibility story will first explain why the client initially hired you and the pain points they were suffering before they hired you. Then, the story will include a short statement about the work you did together, before talking about the happy ending for the client, as a result of using your services.

This is an example of a credibility story.

Example

I was asked to do a supplier exit audit for one of my clients, who suspected that their supplier owed them large amounts of money. As a result of the audit, and the recommendations in my report, my client was able to recover £100,000 of monies owing to them, and also got the supplier to refund my fees.

These credibility stories can be used in your networker's pitch (see Chapter 6), in proposals, presentations, sales meetings, your website, articles and your LinkedIn profile. They can be used as the answer to any of these standard questions that you will receive at a networking event.

- How's business?
- What do you do?
- Got any interesting client work on at the moment?
- What does your firm specialise in?

Your credibility stories will need to be tailored to the document you are writing or for the person you are meeting for the first time. For this reason, you will need a minimum of three credibility stories, which illustrate the type of clients you work with and the value you bring to them.

Case study 1
Adrian Jenkins

Adrian Jenkins is the auditor the big consumer brands turn to when they are concerned that their marketing agencies are mismanaging their money. He identified that potential clients often didn't believe their agencies could be handling their money badly. As a consequence, he built a suite of credibility stories and used them in emails requesting a first meeting with a potential client. These stories have helped him gain a first meeting with 50 per cent of the potential clients he approaches.

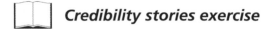 *Credibility stories exercise*

RELATIONSHIP HOOKS

As the saying goes, people still buy from people. When people meet you online or in the flesh, you need to provide clues about you that help the other person get to know you better as a person. These are called relationship hooks. Any lines that you write about yourself, whether in an author credit or your LinkedIn profile, will be built using a mix of credibility statements, credibility stories and relationship hooks.

A relationship hook could be:

- a line in your biography where you mention your hobbies and interests outside of work
- something that shows your personality, such as a particular turn of phrase, an example you use or a testimonial you show
- something about your background, such as where you grew up.

Examples of relationship hooks we have seen used in people's LinkedIn profiles

Jennifer Holloway, author of *Personal Branding for Brits*
With a CV that includes 15 years in PR and media relations, I've learnt a thing or two about promoting a personal brand and managing a reputation – I did it every time I picked up the phone to a journalist.

Katherine Everitt-Newton, resilience coach
As a coach and corporate change agent, I believe that stress is not normal and shouldn't be a part of our everyday routine.

▶

> Roger Hammond, accountant specialising in advising family-owned businesses and charities
> Interestingly, I have always enjoyed working with the practice charity clients and have become the office partner qualified to advise and sign off charities' accounts... Indeed, some may say that I am of a charitable disposition as I have been a lifelong supporter of Everton FC.

 **Relationship hooks exercise**

WEBSITE

Most potential clients expect their professional adviser to have a website or to be mentioned on their firm's website. Before a potential client has contacted you, assume that they have checked this out in advance. Only having an entry in a directory, a LinkedIn profile page or business page on Facebook is not a good substitute for your own website or entry on your firm's website.

Tip

To be seen as a Go-To Expert, your firm's website must list you by name and show your special subject.

Need help with your website?

Helping you decide what to put on your website is beyond the scope of this book. If you need help, we highly recommend you read *Valuable Content Marketing* by Sonja Jefferson and Sharon Tanton, and *Watertight Marketing* by Bryony Thomas.

BLOG

People are more likely to buy from you if they feel that they already 'know' you. By having a blog, which you regularly update, you can build a community of people who know, like and trust you – and want to engage with you. Your blog is an important part of your brand and allows you to showcase your credibility, skills and personality with your potential clients. If your firm won't allow you an entry on their website, then consider setting up your own blog to showcase your talents to potential clients.

Here are examples of good blog sites:

Valuable Content **www.valuablecontent.co.uk**

Principled Selling **www.principledselling.org**

Ian Brodie **www.ianbrodie.com**

In Chapter 5, we talk you through how to use your blog to win business with your target audience.

BUSINESS CARD

A business card is still the world of business's preferred way of exchanging contact details. Most companies will provide their client-facing employees with ones. Remember, there is nothing stopping you from getting your own business card made up. What needs to go on your business card:

- your name, your company name, your job title
- a mailing address – normally now you need include only your email address, rather than your physical address
- phone numbers, preferably a direct line where you can always be reached
- your company logo
- a tagline or description of you and/or your firm
- your website address.

John was a facilitator in the HR department of a medium-sized company, but he wanted to become a Go-To Expert for people seeking a career change. He set up a personal website with his employer's knowledge and negotiated to drop back to a four-day work week, so he could indulge this passion without upsetting anyone.

Tip

Don't choose a glossy or laminate finish for your business card. It may look impressive, but is very hard for people to write on.

The back of your business card is a valuable piece of real estate. You can choose to add the following to the back of it:

- a list of the services that you offer (see Chapter 3)
- a blank space for people to add notes when they meet you
- valuable resources for your niche market
- inspirational images linked to the value you bring.

When buying your business card, do think about the impression you want to give when you hand over your card? A professionally designed, clean, new, high-quality business card will leave a very different impression from a poorly designed, cheaply produced, scuffed, ripped or dirty business card.

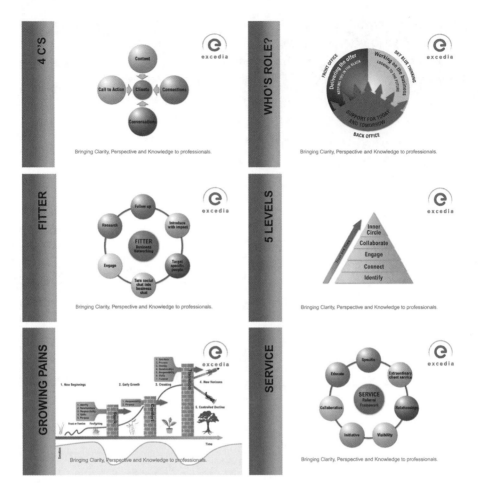

Figure 4.2 The backs of our business cards

Source: Infographics by Angie Phillips, ANG Creative Design

BIOGRAPHIES, INCLUDING YOUR AUTHOR CREDIT, SHORT BIO AND LONG BIO

The purpose of your professional biography (bio) is to help you tell your story in a way that:

- emphasises your credentials
- allows your audience or reader to get to know a bit more about you
- signals aspects that confirm you as a Go-To Expert.

Your author credit is the few lines you write at the bottom of an article, identifying you as the writer of the article. If you submit an article to a publication, you will be expected to include an author credit. Very often an editor will cut your author credit down to fit the word count or editorial policy on author credits.

Examples of author credits

Guy Clapperton became a journalist in the technology press in 1989, going freelance in 1993. He started using early forms of social media almost immediately as his working network. He contributed to many of the national press – still does – and started writing books in the early part of the twenty-first century. At around the same time he added media training to his offerings and in this way is a coach to several clients per month. He regularly speaks on the subject of social media and media in its widest context.

David Tovey is the author of Principled Selling: How to Win More Business Without Selling Your Soul *(published by Kogan Page). He is a business development consultant, coach and speaker with over 20 years' experience of working with professional service firms in the UK and internationally.*

Typically, you will be asked for several different forms of your bio. Often you will hear people referring to your short and long bio. A short bio is a three–five sentence paragraph and is normally used as your author credit, whereas a long bio is, typically, half a page of A4.

Your long bios usually will be composed of a mixture of your sound bite, credibility statements and relationship hooks. For example:

Simon Smith helps professional sportspeople reduce the amount of money they pay in tax to the government [sound bite]. As a former world junior silver medallist and member of the British Athletes Commission Elite Athletes Club [credibility statement], it's no surprise that he has spent the last decade advising over 1,000 professional sportspeople [credibility statement] and is on the Professional Footballers' Association and British Athletes Commission's list of recommended accountants [credibility statement].

Simon won two silver medals at the world junior championships for long jump [credibility statement]. He qualified to go to the Beijing Olympics, but then unfortunately suffered a career-ending injury [relationship hook]. A passion for problemsolving, combined with the stability of a career in accountancy, was what initially drew Simon to the world of tax [relationship hook]. It then became only a small 'jump' for Simon to specialise in helping his former team-mates and other professional sportspeople with their tax affairs.

Simon's current client list of over 150 clients includes 10+ UK Olympic medal winners and over 15 current and retired professional footballers [credibility statement]. Many of his clients come to him via his current clients, because 'he really does understand what it is like to be in the world of sport' [credibility statement].

Simon regularly writes about tax matters for professional sportspeople and is often asked to speak at sports industry conferences and events [credibility statement]. One place you wouldn't find him now is at the athletics stadium – his two young sons would much prefer that he kicks a football around with them at the local park [relationship hook].

First or third person?

A professional bio written for a social media profile is normally written in the first person, as it is believed that this makes you seem friendlier and more approachable. By contrast, a professional bio written for a magazine, brochure, programme or proposal is normally written in the third person, as this is perceived to be more 'businesslike'.

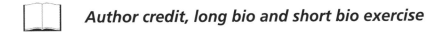 *Author credit, long bio and short bio exercise*

ONE-PAGE CREDENTIALS DOCUMENT

This is a one-page document that gives prospective clients the following:

- your sound bite, i.e. who you are and who you work for
- your short bio
- typical types of projects or assignments you undertake

- your client list
- short client testimonials
- contact details.

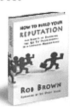

Who Is Rob Brown?

Rob Brown is a world leading authority on networking and business relationships. He is author of over 50 publications, including the bestseller **How to Build Your Reputation.**

Rob is Head of the **Global Networking Council,** featuring the world's greatest networking thinkers, authors and experts. He hosts the online **Networking Giants Radio Show** with these gurus on the topics of business networking, online networking, persuasion, influence, relationship capital, trust, connecting, word of mouth and referrals.

He coaches and trains business professionals around the world to network more profitably, generate high quality referrals and become the number one choice for what they do in a crowded marketplace.

BORN in 1965, Rob grew up in Hull, Yorkshire (UK). In his early days travelled extensively around the USA, Australia and Europe. In 1992, he qualified as a joint Mathematics and Phys Ed teacher, showing big kids how to do tough sums, pass exams, play football and throw javelins!

From 1993-1996, he lived the 'expat life' in Hong Kong, doing acting, coaching and teaching in an international school. After a 'religious experience' in Charlotte, North Carolina (USA), he returned to the UK in 1996 to continue his teaching career. In 1999 he began a Masters in Human Resource Development before taking a sales role in the global health care company BUPA. To grow his business, Rob went networking. During a period of two years, he collected 987 business cards, went to 126 events, spent 200 hours shaking hands and £4385 on breakfasts, lunches, dinners and memberships.

He won NO business! All he was earning was commission on a few company leads. Rob reached a critical point of 'financial urgency' where he knew something had to change. He resolved to become an expert at networking. It prompted him to learn everything he could on marketing and business relationships. What happened next?

In just 13 months, he multiplied his income by a factor of 15!

People soon began asking Rob how he did it! So in 2004, he founded his own networking company specialising in showing people how to network productively and stand out a crowd. Rob is now the UK's most recommended person on Linkedin, and the most recommended networking guru on Linkedin in the world!

Rob lives in Nottingham, England (home of Robin Hood) with his wife Amanda, and two daughters Georgia and Madison. In his spare time, Rob likes kick-boxing, juggling, chess, backgammon, playing guitar, learning jazz piano and watching movies. He loves milk chocolate but not alcohol, grapefruit and inconsiderate drivers! A committed Christian and philanthropist, Rob has a life vision to give away £1m to Christian causes. He's a few thousand short at the moment, but working on it!

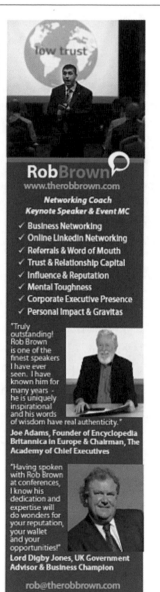

RobBrown
www.therobbrown.com

*Networking Coach
Keynote Speaker & Event MC*

✓ Business Networking
✓ Online Linkedin Networking
✓ Referrals & Word of Mouth
✓ Trust & Relationship Capital
✓ Influence & Reputation
✓ Mental Toughness
✓ Corporate Executive Presence
✓ Personal Impact & Gravitas

"Truly outstanding! Rob Brown is one of the finest speakers I have ever seen. I have known him for many years - he is uniquely inspirational and his words of wisdom have real authenticity."

Joe Adams, Founder of Encyclopedia Britannica in Europe & Chairman, The Academy of Chief Executives

"Having spoken with Rob Brown at conferences, I know his dedication and expertise will do wonders for your reputation, your wallet and your opportunities!"

Lord Digby Jones, UK Government Advisor & Business Champion

rob@therobbrown.com

Rob Brown with former South Africa President FW de Clerk

Rob Brown with Charlie Duke, one of the few men to land on the moon

Figure 4.3 Example of a one-page credentials document[1]
Source: www.therobbrown.com

[1] For the most up-to-date version go to **www.therobbrown.com/onepage**

PROFESSIONAL PHOTOS

You will, at some point in time, be asked to provide photos of yourself. They could be for:

- your website
- an avatar for social media
- a proposal
- publicity
- an article you have written
- an event you are going to be speaking at.

Typically, you will need two different photos. Your head and shoulders, then a full-length photo of you for publicity purposes. It is worth engaging a photographer who specialises in portraiture to take these photos for you. These photos will follow you everywhere in your career, so it is worth the time and investment to get them just right.

A good professional photo will:

- capture your best side
- be properly lit and processed to showcase you rather than the background
- represent the brand or image you want to portray
- will not have you square on to the camera
- make you feel good about yourself.

SPEAKER KIT

In order to generate bookings as a speaker, typically you will require the following within your personal marketing kit.

- Short video clips of you in action. These video clips ideally need to give any potential event organisers a flavour of what you talk about, as well as your ability to engage and entertain your audience.
- A one-page or speaker sheet, which gives details of your credibility, how to get in contact, your photo, details of your webpage, the topics you speak on, plus your main keynotes.

For a comprehensive example of a speaking kit, see Rob Brown's speaking page: **www.therobbrown.com/book-rob-brown**

See Chapter 8 for more details of what should be included in your speaker kit.

SOCIAL MEDIA PROFILES

At the time of writing, Go-To Experts have a vast array of social networking sites on which to maintain a presence. Typically, the four on which you should be active are LinkedIn, Twitter, Facebook and Google+.

For example, LinkedIn is great for meeting corporate decisionmakers and joining sector-specific groups; Twitter is a great place to keep up to date with what is going on, plus meet and form relationships with journalists; Facebook is excellent for keeping in touch with current and ex-colleagues; Google+ is rapidly growing and maintaining a presence is essential to help you increase your search engine rankings.

> *"If you are looking to broaden your reputation within an industry or within a target group, relying exclusively on doing it face-to-face, rather than using a mix of online and face-to-face, is a very slow and expensive way to do it."*
>
> LEE FREDERIKSEN, MANAGING PARTNER, HINGE, AND CO-AUTHOR OF
> *PROFESSIONAL SERVICES MARKETING*

With all the work you have completed on your credibility statements, credibility stories and bios, plus your photo, you now have all the material you need at your fingertips to fill in your profiles on these social networking sites.

Tips for filling out your profiles

- Do upload your photo to your profile. You will seem more credible and authentic with a photo than without.
- Remember to include important keywords in your profiles, as very often your clients will search for someone like you using keywords.

- Don't leave your profile blank, as this will result in people assuming that you are not a Go-To Expert on anything.
- Include links to your social media profiles on the bottom of your emails.

For more help on what to put in your LinkedIn, Twitter, Facebook and Google+ profile, visit **www.joinedupnetworking.com/category/on-line-networking-2**

NAME BADGE

Getting your own name badge made for when you are out networking is a good investment. Your own badge typically will set you back under £10 and it will help you present a professional image when you meet people at events. Unlike many of the badges handed out at events, yours will:

- be spelt correctly
- have the right details and branding
- always be with you
- not damage or dirty your suit like a stick-on label.

TEMPLATES FOR SLIDES, DOCUMENTS AND HANDOUTS

It's often the little things that can break or damage your reputation as the Go-To Expert. One of these little things can be as simple as the look and feel of written material that you share with people.

A graphic designer can create a set of templates based on the brand and image you want to consistently present to the outside world. Having these set up as standard templates can save huge amounts of time in the future.

PRESS KIT

This is simply a pack of material about you and your business, which the media will find useful to write stories about you, find out more about you or feature you in an article. Your press kit is like your professional resumé and will contain most of the items in your personal marketing toolkit.

VIDEOS OF YOU

Watching you talk, present or do a showcase on video can help your prospects get to know you and build trust and credibility before you speak or meet in person. YouTube is the second-biggest search engine after Google and many of your potential clients will use it to find advice.

Tips for using video

- If you are being videoed at an event, always ask for a copy of 'your bit'.
- Go for the highest production quality and value you can afford for your video, especially if you are wanting to put together a speaker's show reel.
- If video blogging, do think about what is going on behind you and around you and look into the camera.

For a good example of the use of video see Guy Clapperton talking about 'making business sense of social media' at **www. youtube.com/watch?list=PLBA16FDA622691F27&feature=player_ embedded&v=mtgdXWMtnu0#at=21**

CLIENT LIST, TESTIMONIALS AND CASE STUDIES

Without breaking client confidentiality, these will show future clients who you have been working with and the types of results you have achieved. On a website, they will help generate new client enquiries.

To increase the impact of your case studies and testimonials, ask your clients if they are happy to be recorded on video.

How to dress the part

The way you dress also communicates a message about you. Whether you agree with it or not, your personal appearance will be judged as an expression of who you are and your approach to the job.

Case study 3
David

David was an up-and-coming partner in a large law firm. He received feedback that he was perceived to lack gravitas because of how he dressed. This *lack of gravitas* was blocking his career progression to partner. After spending time with an image consultant, he made over his work wardrobe. Within 18 months of his makeover, he was promoted to partner, at the first time of asking.

Your hair, shoes, tattoos, piercings and clothes will be taken as indicators of your status, self-confidence, self-care and self-worth. If you get your image right, it is likely to be noticed but not commented on. If you get your image wrong, then this will damage your credibility and hamper you on your way to becoming the Go-To Expert. Very often, you wouldn't get told directly that you are dressing inappropriately, because many people shy away from this kind of conversation as it feels far too personal and too risky.

Tip

Dressing the part doesn't mean you will automatically progress, but not dressing the part will definitely hinder career advancement in professional services firms.

If you are getting feedback similar to that listed below, then it is likely you need to spend some time considering how to change your look at work:

- lacks presence, charisma or gravitas
- doesn't look the part
- isn't polished enough.

17 tips to help you strengthen your presence, not detract from it

1 Dress for the reputation you want. Look at how the successful people in your industry dress and, as much as you feel comfortable with, copy their style.

2 Do not wear clothes that are considered to be too revealing, tight or short.

3 Keep your wardrobe updated and regularly ditch anything that has become worn, stained, ripped or tired.

4 Do add new items to your professional wardrobe at least once a year.

5 Don't become a fashion victim, but keep an eye out for what styles are current and, most importantly, be conscious of what's not.

6 Invest in classic pieces for your wardrobe that will never go out of fashion.

7 Make sure your clothes fit properly.

8 Consider investing more in key pieces of clothes that are made to measure for you.

9 Don't dress for comfort, dress for presence. For example, walk to work in comfortable trainers, but immediately change into work shoes when you enter your office.

10 Always aim to dress slightly more formally than your clients. For example, if your clients dress casually in jeans, then dress in business casual when you go to see them.

11 Always have a comb and mirror handy before you go and meet clients or go to an important meeting.

▶

12 Always have a jacket in the office in case you need to dress up an outfit or a client unexpectedly visits.

13 Wear clothes that cover up any visible tattoos.

14 Keep your nails and hands neat and tidy.

15 Remove any excessive facial or ear piercings.

16 Men, keep your facial hair tidy and neatly groomed.

17 Always check your back view in the mirror before leaving home or going into a meeting – you should be aware what others are seeing when you exit a meeting while they remain. For this reason, it's worth polishing the backs of your shoes as well as the fronts.

Social media etiquette

Your usage of social media will dominate your online footprint and the first impression you make when meeting people online. Get this wrong and you could easily damage your credibility. Here are some dos and don'ts to make sure social media works for you rather than against you.

DO

- Engage in conversation rather than solely broadcasting your thoughts, content and own material.
- Be polite and remember your manners. You don't know who could be listening to your conversation.
- Try to be helpful rather than just pushing your own opinion or services.
- Think before you post anything online: is this helping me build a strong and positive reputation?
- Speak to someone online as if they were standing next to you.
- Apologise if you receive negative comments online and offer to take the conversation offline.

- Remember that everyone is entitled to an opinion and you can't please everyone all the time.
- Let your personality shine through, but don't go off-message.
- Hang out online where your target audience hangs out.

DON'T

- Swear, moan or whine.
- Post online when excessively tired or drunk.
- Post anything you wouldn't be happy for your mother, a journalist, boss or good friend to read .
- Fight out your personal or professional battles on social media.
- Share everything about your life, warts and all. Some things are best left unsaid!
- Be completely black and white with your opinions or thoughts – always leave room for some grey areas.

Summary

Creating the right first impression, both online and offline, is vital if you are to be seen and talked about as the Go-To Expert. To help make that all-important first impression, you will need consistent messages about you, which emphasise your authority and the results that you help your clients achieve. Typically, these messages are formed from your credibility statements, credibility stories and relationship hooks.

To help you keep the messages consistent, and to save time, it is worthwhile putting together a personal marketing toolkit.

Action points

1 Think about the top three pain points, why your clients would want to work with you. For each pain point write a credibility story to show how you have helped a client eliminate this pain point.

2 Ask for feedback from some trusted peers on how you come across in person and online. Make changes based on their suggestions.

3 Go to the websites of three people you consider to be Go-To Experts in any field. See if you can identify one good thing that they do and copy or adopt their style.

4 Fill in your LinkedIn/Twitter/Facebook/Google+ profile(s) using the credibility statements, credibility stories and bios you have written.

5 Hire a graphic designer to produce a set of branded templates for articles, white papers, reports, business cards, email footers, etc.

6 Get a set of professional photos taken of you to use for publicity, PR and social media.

Further resources

For help thinking through what you want and need in your personal marketing kit, we recommend these resources.

BOOKS

- Brown, R. (2007) *How to Build Your Reputation: The secrets of becoming the 'go to' professional in a crowded marketplace*, Penryn: Ecademy Press

- Holloway, J. (2013) *Personal Branding for Brits: A practical guide to blowing your own trumpet without sounding like an eejit*, Skipton: Spark Ltd

- Jefferson, S. and Tanton, S. (2013) *Valuable Content Marketing: How to make quality content the key to your business success*, London: Kogan Page

- Thomas, B. (2013) *Watertight Marketing: Delivering long-term sales results*, St Albans: Anoma Press

WEBSITES

- Joined Up Networking **www.joinedupnetworking.com/ category/on-line-networking-2**
- How to make partner **www.howtomakepartner.com/ category/building-your-portfolio/developing-your-brand/ branding-yourself**
- Valuable Content **www.valuablecontent.co.uk**
- Spark – personal branding for business **www.sparkexec.co.uk**
- *Watertight Marketing* **www.watertightmarketing.com**

5

How to use your content to reinforce your expertise

Topics covered in this chapter.

- What is meant by valuable content?
- The three ways to create your content.
- What is a content plan?
- Questions to ask before writing a content plan.
- Planning your business development content.
- Tips to save time producing and sharing content.
- The how, what, when and why of blogging.

As the status of being the Go-To Expert suggests, you will benefit from the luxury of having clients who choose to come and find you, thus negating the need for you to go out and sell to them. To do this, you will need to continually find and write valuable content, then share it with your target audience. This chapter helps you identify what content your clients will find valuable.

"If you continually share information that people actually value, clients and customers will choose to come to you."

SONJA JEFFERSON AND SHARON TANTON, AUTHORS OF
VALUABLE CONTENT MARKETING

What is meant by valuable content?

"Valuable content is the focus of all good marketing today."

CHARLES H. GREEN, CO-AUTHOR OF *THE TRUSTED ADVISOR*
AND *TRUST-BASED SELLING*

Content is any information you have written, videoed, recorded or shared e.g.:

- white paper
- blog post
- article in press

- quote in an article
- YouTube video
- podcast
- comment in LinkedIn discussion
- tweet
- webinar
- book
- page on your website.

Anyone can write and share content, whereas valuable content is anything you share that your target audience will find valuable. For example, if you are an intellectual property (IP) lawyer for coaches and trainers, a valuable piece of content for them would be bespoke tips to help them protect their IP.

The internet has permanently changed how people buy professional services. Only ten years ago, all you had to do to become the Go-To Expert was get your name in the right place – write a book, regularly speak at events, have a three-page brochure and use a sales team to follow up any telephone, email or postal enquiries. Today's modern world moves at such a pace that clients want answers now – not three days later, not at next month's event. This is why people turn to the internet first to get answers to questions, problems, challenges and opportunities.

> *"Content marketing, i.e. producing a steady stream of helpful content to your audience, distributed through social media, is the quickest way for a professional to establish their reputation."*
>
> LEE FREDERIKSEN, MANAGING PARTNER, HINGE, AND CO-AUTHOR OF
> *PROFESSIONAL SERVICES MARKETING*

Another consequence of our time-poor lifestyle is our reduced tolerance for old-style marketing, i.e. the 'buy this now' message just doesn't work. We want to take the sales process at our pace, not the adviser's pace. We want to be able to do some of our own research, rather than rely on what the adviser is telling us. The answer to the marketing conundrum faced by all professionals is valuable content, i.e. content that will inform, help, entertain and provoke our target audience. As Sonja Jefferson and Sharon Tanton in their book *Valuable Content Marketing* said:

"If you regularly share this type of information you will draw people to your business – the company that inspires, understands and offers clear answers is the obvious place to turn when the time comes to buy."

As the Go-To Expert you will need to build up a library of valuable content that helps you get found, emphasises your credibility for what you do and systemises how you work with clients. Your content splits into two broad categories:

- content that helps to find, attract and retain clients, e.g. a blog post that helps your niche market solve a problem they have
- content that helps you work with clients more efficiently and effectively, e.g. a standard template for your client engagement letters.

Case study 1
Hinge Marketing

Hinge Marketing is a US marketing agency specialising in working with professional service firms. They regularly produce and share freely valuable content, such as books, weekly webinars, reports, blog posts, via their social media channels and mailing list. They got a call from a local firm with a request for a proposal to help them rebrand their firm. At the time the firm was on their database, but they didn't know anyone at the firm. Against their better judgement they submitted a proposal and won the work without meeting them. They found out later that the firm had done a full request for proposals and got in multiple potential suppliers and interviewed these suppliers. They asked their new client why they were successful rather than any of the other suppliers. Their client had been following them for two years and had developed a strong trust in their credibility through the content they regularly shared. Because they had this trust and sense of relationship, they didn't feel it was necessary to actually meet with them in person during the tendering process.

The three ways to create your content

The biggest barrier professionals have to sustainably producing valuable content is time. However, with planning, it is possible to efficiently produce content.

GENERATE

This is content that you have created from scratch. This could include:

- blog posts written from scratch and not adapted from anywhere else
- updates on LinkedIn, Twitter and Facebook where you post where you are, what you are thinking, what you are about to do, or pose a question to your followers
- white papers, reports, guides, workbooks, etc.
- video interviews with your fee earners
- conversations on Twitter and internet forums
- standard forms, questionnaires, methodologies for the work you do with clients.

RECYCLE

This is repurposed or repacked content, which you have adapted from its original form. This could include:

- recycling a piece of work you do for a client to use with others
- publishing (with permission) another person's blog post on your blog (which they have already published elsewhere) or vice versa
- repackaging a white paper or report into several blog posts
- creating a standard questionnaire to use with other clients based on a piece of client work you have just done
- adapting a plan from a contact in a totally different industry to suit your own purposes.

CURATE

This is where you filter or select/share other people's or your firm's content that you think your network, contacts, clients or social media followers will find valuable. This could include:

- tweeting a link to a blog post or article (whether or not it is your own article)
- retweeting someone else's content
- sharing a link to a blog or article on LinkedIn
- including copies of presentations, video clips, white papers, reports and guides on fee earners' LinkedIn profiles
- sending out a valuable article to targeted people in your network
- creating a discussion on a LinkedIn group based on the key points contained in an article
- using a newsletter to share interesting articles on a theme.

What is a content plan?

A content plan is where you develop a framework for the valuable content you will produce.

WHY IS IT USEFUL?

A content plan helps you to think about and schedule your content in advance. This has many benefits, including:

- allowing you to align your content production with your marketing plans, particularly campaigns
- saving time, as you are not thinking about what you need to write all the time
- enabling you to ask other people to write the content you need, for the time you need it.

MONTH	JAN	FEB	MAR
GUIDES, REPORTS, WHITE PAPERS	Guide to tax planning for solicitor practices	Decisions needed in order to bring in a new equity partner	Tips for successful mergers
BLOG POSTS	Seven ways to minimise tax bill Case study on client	Six tips to make a good lateral hire Ten tips to grow your own equity partners Case study on client	Ten ways to merge your firm successfully Case study on client
NEWSLETTER	Focused on saving tax	Focused on how to bring in new equity partner	Focused on issues surrounding merging firm
LINKEDIN	New blog status updates Discussions based around new blog posts	New blog status updates Discussions based around new blog posts	New blog status updates Discussions based around new blog posts
TWITTER	Practice management tips for solicitor firms Links to blog posts Links to articles in *Legal Week* and *The Lawyer*	Practice management tips for solicitor firms Links to blog posts Links to articles in *Legal Week* and *The Lawyer*	Practice management tips for solicitor firms Links to blog posts Links to articles in *Legal Week* and *The Lawyer*

Figure 5.1 Example of a content plan

HOW DO YOU BUILD A CONTENT PLAN?

Typically, your content plan will be split into two areas:

- business development content
- business processes content.

Examples of business development content include:

- guides, reports, blog posts and white papers that help to demonstrate credibility
- briefing documents for potential clients to help reduce the perceived barriers and risks to hiring you
- published and self-published books and e-books

- incentives for people to sign up to the mailing list on your website
- podcasts, videos, YouTube clips, recorded teleseminars and webinars
- case studies, testimonials
- things that can be sold to clients or bundled to increase the perceived value of your service or product
- autoresponder sequences for when people sign up to your list
- LinkedIn, Tweets or Facebook status updates
- answers on internet forums
- contributions to discussion threads on internet forums
- comments on other people's blog posts
- newsletters
- weekly tips sent out by email.

Examples of business processes content include:

- engagement letters
- terms and conditions
- new client forms
- new client welcome packs
- fact-finding questionnaires
- standard report templates
- standard emails to support internal/external processes.

NB: Deciding on content to help you run your part of the practice more efficiently is beyond the scope of this book.

Questions to ask before writing a content plan

Before jumping into writing a content plan, it is always worth taking a step back, to think about some important questions that will help you and/or your firm save time in the long run.

- What is a realistic expectation for your ongoing content creation?
- Where are your clients looking for information?
- What sorts of questions or problems are your clients looking to the firm to answer?
- What content can be created by you, other people in the firm and by outside (independent) sources?
- What infrastructure (e.g. blog, email marketing software) do you have available to help deliver the content?

Planning your business development content

"Many professionals write boring technical articles, when really they should be starting with the simple things which worry their typical clients."

ALAN STEVENS, AUTHOR OF *PING, THE POCKET MEDIA COACH* AND CO-AUTHOR OF *MEDIA MASTERS*

The purpose of this type of content is to help you find, sign up and keep clients. Each new client you sign up typically will go through a similar process, often referred to as the marketing and sales funnel.[2] Your business development content will keep the right prospects and clients in the funnel and progress them through from a prospect to a loyal client.

"Powerful content helps your audience understand who you are, and what your approach is to things. It is not self-serving or sales copy, but content which educates them, informs them and helps them understand the challenges they may be facing."

LEE FREDERIKSEN, MANAGING PARTNER, HINGE, AND CO-AUTHOR OF *PROFESSIONAL SERVICES MARKETING*

Let's look at each stage in the marketing and sales funnel.

---

[2] The marketing and sales funnel is adapted from Dr Philip Kotler's rational decisionmaking models.

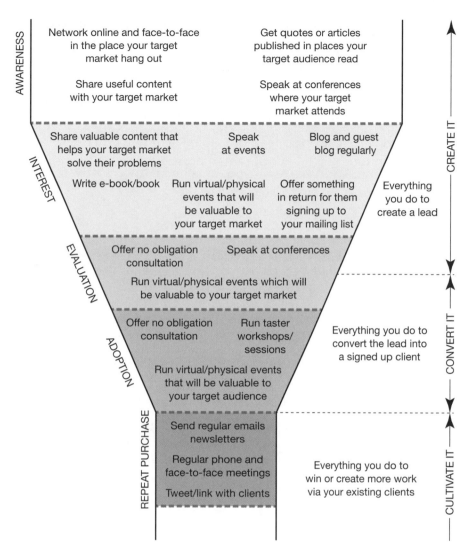

Figure 5.2 The marketing and sales funnel, with ideas of what you could be doing at each stage of the funnel to help progress someone to become a loyal client

CREATE IT

This is everything you do to generate a lead, i.e. a genuine prospect that has made contact with you about using your services. For example:

- write valuable content that builds your profile and visibility with your target audience

- share your valuable content in places where it is most visible to your target audience, as well as people in your network who can introduce you to potential clients
- use your content to show your target audience that you can help them with their challenges and requirements, and you truly walk your walk and talk your talk
- provide a steady drip feed of valuable content and use it to stay in touch with your potential prospects until they are ready to buy.

CONVERT IT

This is everything that you do to convert the lead into a signed-up client who has paid their first invoice.

- Assist with qualifying the enquiry you have received – is it the sort of client you want to work with?
- Anticipate and overcome any objections that clients may have to working with you.
- Build confidence in your business in the eyes of potential clients.
- Provide a steady drip feed of valuable content and use it to stay in touch with your potential prospects until they are ready to buy.

CULTIVATE IT

This is everything you do to win more work from your existing clients, either through them recommending you to others or buying more services from you. Therefore, you need to create valuable content that:

- is written and presented in such a manner that current clients will feel it is easy to forward the content on to other people
- keeps clients interested by demonstrating how you are leading change and advancing your expertise
- maintains a high level of client service, even if your current engagement has finished.

Case study 2
James

James is an employment law partner in a large legal firm and specialises in the hospitality sector.

He thinks about his clients in terms of the three stages they might be in: unknowns, potentials and current clients. He prepares valuable content materials for those groups.

For the unknowns, he writes a 'Simple guide to hiring temporary staff and avoiding the pitfalls', which is actually in eight parts so that he can drip feed this to his target audience. The parts appear in his blog and he also places some in a trade magazines.

James also arranges for these eight parts to be featured in an accountant's regular newsletter to its hospitality clients. They told him that they were willing to help because the content was so valuable. Importantly, what he had written was not blatantly pushing his services, but they did give his name and contact details at the bottom.

For the potentials, he wrote a longer set of articles, many of which gave case studies showing how to get more value for money from your agency staff. To access these articles, the readers needed to click through to his website and sign up for his free weekly email tip. Again, James was determined not to 'sell', but, rather, offer valuable information.

Realising that some clients wanted to 'see' James rather than read articles written by him, James sourced YouTube clips to

▶

make for more compelling content. Some were from the internet and some others were testimonials from clients he videoed himself. As he was behind the camera, the cost of producing these testimonials was low.

Finally, for his existing clients, he wanted them to stay with him and talk about his services to others. He did some proprietary research into the most cost-effective way for hospitality companies to recruit agency staff. He shared this information with his current clients and invited them to bring along a guest to a seminar he was hosting to discuss the implications of his research for them.

Tips to save time producing and sharing content

Here are some tips we use to save time producing and distributing content:

- schedule or automate the everyday content that you share on social media as much as possible, using tools such as Hootsuite, Twitterfeed and Bufferapp
- get into the routine of checking in on your key social media sites daily
- aim to engage fully with a handful of sites rather than barely engaging with many sites, groups and communities
- plan to write 80 per cent of your blog posts in advance, before your planned publish date
- use the 'Favorites' function on Twitter to build up a store of useful content to share via Bufferapp across your social media profiles.

The how, what, when and why of blogging

One of the key pieces of infrastructure for your valuable content is your blog and it is important to maximise the effectiveness of the blog.

WHAT IS BLOGGING?

A blog is a form of website where you can self-publish articles without needing the approval of anyone else. Your content plan will guide what content you need to write about and your blogging schedule.

A blog post is not like a magazine article or feature. It is often shorter and more informal in nature than these types of articles. The ideal length of a blog post is 200 to 500 words, i.e. long enough to provide something of value, but short enough to be digested in 5 to 10 minutes.

Unlike traditional printed newspapers and magazines, anyone can start a blog. There are many free blogging tools, e.g. WordPress.com, or Blogger, that will allow you to set up a free account in minutes and start blogging. It is recommended that you host your blog on a platform that you control, i.e. within your own website. That way you will be able to keep an eye on all of your content.

The point of a blog is to help people see past the commercial literature and help connect with you as a person, i.e. your personal brand. Your blog is a great tool to build up trust and credibility with your target audience, showing you understand them and you know what you are talking about.

BENEFITS OF BLOGGING

A blog is a fantastic destination point to showcase your credibility and demonstrate your thought-leadership to your target audience, as well as keep in touch with your existing network and clients. When your niche market 'meets' you in the online world, it is often interested to know whether you are the real deal or not. A well-maintained blog – which you direct people to read either via Twitter or a link on a forum post – is the easiest way to build up your credibility and strengthen your online personal brand.

Your page rank on Google is heavily influenced by how much fresh content you have on your website. As a blog is dynamic – users can interact with the website – Google is likely to place a greater weight on a blog than on a static website. This means that maintaining a keyword-rich blog is vital for effective search engine optimisation. Owning a website that features highly in the search engine ranking is a way of generating a readymade interested audience to network with you.

Case study 3
Martin Bragg

When Martin, a business development expert for professional service firms, knew his role at a top five accountancy practice was coming to an end, he set about raising his profile and building the size and quality of his network to improve his future employability. Using LinkedIn, he sent tailored personal emails and made contact with more than 25 high-profile members of professional services. Everyone he contacted ended up connecting to him and Martin built on these connections to have calls or face-to-face meetings with the vast majority.

As a result of the relationships he built, he was invited to do some guest blogging for a number of these people. He noticed that every time a guest blog of his was published, the number of views of his LinkedIn profile increased by a factor of up to four or more. It was as a result of his increased profile, due to his guest blogging, that he was headhunted to head up a business development function for a law firm in the Middle East.

BLOG SITE VERSUS WEBSITE?

When people talk about a blog site, they normally are referring to websites where the blog part of the website is at the front of the site and the brochure part of the website is at the back. A website is where the brochure part of the website is at the front of the website and it may or may not have a blog either integrated within the site or a link to the company's blog hosted on a different domain or sub-domain.

To help you understand what you need for your website, here are a few questions and pointers.

The first question is very simple: when did you last willingly read some marketing collateral, be it an advert or brochure website? I'm guessing the answer is, or was (unless you were doing competitor research), probably a long time ago. You are not an isolated case. We all now have so much access to information that we are tuning out marketing spin and becoming much more selective over what we read and when we will read it.

Now translate this to your website: if all you are doing is shoving marketing hype at your potential clients (i.e. website visitors), then how willing are they going to be to engage with what you are writing or return at a later date? Add to this the fact that most of your potential clients are not ready to buy at the point they visit your website for the first time.

So, the million-dollar question is, how do you encourage these potential clients and advocates to regularly visit your website so that, when they are ready to buy, you – rather than your competitors – are top of their minds and the person who gets the phone call?

Before answering this question, let's look at two other important ingredients in the buying criteria for professional services – trust and credibility. Anyone can stick up a website saying they are great and get a friendly client or two to supply some nicely worded testimonials. Most people have realised this and want to have more proof of your expertise to be able to solve their problems.

This is where the power of a blog site comes in. It helps professional advisers maintain, in a time and cost-effective way, trust and credibility and visibility with their current and potential clients. Your blog provides a wealth of valuable content to your potential clients, which demonstrates your expertise in your chosen specialist area. Remember, to get the desired benefits from your blog, you will need to have well-thought out content and regularly update it.

You have a choice – do you hide your blog at the back of your website – i.e. a couple of clicks away – or do you feature it on the prime real estate of your homepage?

Figure 5.3 Example of a good homepage

Source: www.venture-now.com

My suggestion is that you bring your content to the front of your website and adopt the blog site approach. Why? Your homepage is the most visited page of the whole of your website. So, provide valuable content at the most commonly used entry point to your website. This will encourage people in and help engage them with the content, thus building your credibility in the process. They are then far more likely to revisit your website, building the relationship further. The more times they return – which a regularly updated blog will encourage them to do – the more likely they will subscribe willingly to your mailing list and use or recommend your services in the future.

You may be thinking that, if it was this simple, why do so many people not have a blog site? This is due partly to a hangover from traditional marketing. Many marketing specialists try to use old marketing techniques in the social media world. Very often this approach doesn't work. Why hide your valuable content away at the back of your website, if this is the very mechanism that is going to positively influence potential clients to buy from you? It doesn't make sense. However, to truly embrace a blog site takes a leap of faith, which many professionals (and business owners, let's be honest) are not yet convinced enough to make.

HOW TO MAXIMISE YOUR EFFECTIVENESS WITH BLOGGING

Writing blog posts can suck away your valuable time. When writing a blog your aim is to make each word count. Here are ways in which you can do that.

1 Use a content plan to work to a schedule, so you are never stuck for words and can repackage your blog post as articles to be used in your business development processes.
2 Identify pain points for your target audience and use these as themes across the year for your content plan.
3 Integrate your blogging with your keep-in-touch strategy.
4 Use your blog posts to educate your potential clients and existing clients on what they should be talking to you about.

5 Use Google analytics to help you track what subjects people are most interested in and use this knowledge to influence your content plan.

6 Ask your clients what they are interested in finding out about at the moment.

Case study 4
Jean

Jean is a partner in a mid-tier firm of accountants who specialises in helping to advise family-owned groups of companies. She saved one of her clients £8 million in inheritance tax. (She also got permission from the client to blog about how they managed it.)

Once she had written the blog post, she started to spread the content via social media and included a link to the blog post on her email footer.

She then went through her client, intermediaries and prospect lists and found people who might have an interest in inheritance tax planning. She sent a personalised email to each of these people, sharing the blog post with them, and asked them if they or their clients had thought much about inheritance tax planning.

HOW OFTEN SHOULD YOU BLOG?

Many people ask this question. The right answer is depends on how often your niche audience expects to read your blog. For example, some professionals blog a couple of times a day, but post up short sharp posts and other professionals write in-depth articles weekly. If you have never blogged before, our suggestion is that you commit to writing a 400-word blog post fortnightly and then increase this to weekly as you get more confident and comfortable with writing blog posts.

> **Tip**
>
> Everything you blog about must be valuable to the reader. The best test of value is if the reader forwards the blog link to other people. To that end, blogging about your office relocation or the Christmas party is not valuable to the external world.

---

16 ideas for what you can blog about

1 Case studies.
2 Testimonials received from happy clients.
3 Achievements of happy clients.
4 What a client or you learnt whilst working together.
5 Interviews with experts inside and outside of your firm.
6 How to articles.
7 Introductions to new team members.
8 Responses to news items or articles.
9 Anything that highlights your personal credentials.
10 Book reviews.
11 Presentations you have prepared.
12 Proposals you have prepared.
13 Video clips of you presenting at a seminar or conference.
14 Any training events that you attend.
15 New products or services that you are starting to sell.
16 Thought for the day.

THE IMPORTANCE OF YOUR BLOG POST'S TITLE

People will make a decision to click through and read your blog post based on your post's title. This means that the headline of your blog post is, in one sense, more important than the actual content of the blog. To influence a person to click through and actually read your blog post, a title either needs to promise value to the reader or pique their curiosity. A compelling title will help your article get noticed by an editor or guest blogger, who may request to use your content on their site.

Titles that help your blog post get more clicks normally fall into the following categories:

- clearly state what the post will deliver in the title, e.g. 'Six tips to avoid stirring up trouble on social media'
- promises to help people save money or time, e.g. 'Simple ways all business owners can legally minimise their tax bill'
- has a counter-intuitive title, e.g. a Chartered Institute of Personnel and Development (CIPD) newsletter article titled 'Why you shouldn't renew your CIPD membership'
- scares your niche market, e.g. 'Are you legally signing people up to your mailing list?'
- includes your target audience's name in the title, e.g. 'Money laundering – what every business owner needs to know to keep safe and legal'.

Summary

Effective use of content will be a key differentiator that helps you market and sell yourself, as well as run your business effectively. Marketing with valuable content is a smart way to get yourself found, build relationships with your network and clients, and win business – without the need for aggressive selling.

Take the time to use a content plan to schedule what you will generate, recycle and curate. This will help you stay on track with your content marketing, regardless of the workload on your desk.

Your blog will probably be one of your most important content tools. It will help you build an emotional connection with your network and, if used strategically, will be one of the best work-winning tools you can use within your business.

Action points

1 Find out three things your competitors are doing online that is better than you and design actions to go one better than them. Then take that action!

2 Complete the content plan: business development exercise in your Go-To Expert Workbook.

3 Find six blogs that you like and enjoy reading. Notice what you like about them and how they use their blogs. Decide what bits are good and take action to improve yours.

4 Ask your clients which blogs they read regularly, why they find them valuable and then make some decisions and take action with your own blog.

5 Find three well-written blogs aimed at your niche market and regularly read them and comment on the blog posts.

6 Start your own blog or start contributing to your firm's blog. Write a schedule for the blog posts you will write over the next one to three months.

Further resources

For help to think through what content you want to use to develop your practice, we recommend these resources.

BOOKS

- Brogan, C. and Smith, J. (2010) *Trust Agents: Using the Web to Build Influence, Improve Reputation, and Earn Trust*, Hoboken, NJ: John Wiley & Sons

- Jefferson, S. and Tanton, S. (2013) *Valuable Content Marketing: How to Make Quality Content the Key to Your Business Success*, London: Kogan Page

- Thomas, B. (2013) *Watertight Marketing: Delivering Long-Term Sales Results*, St Albans: Anoma Press

For help with starting a blog or winning business from your blog, we recommend these books:

- Rowse, D. and Garrett, C. (2012) *ProBlogger: Secrets for blogging your way to a six-figure income*, Indianapolis, IN: John Wiley & Sons
- Thewlis, P. (2008) *WordPress for business bloggers*, Birmingham: PACKT Publishing
- Townsend, H. (2011) *The Financial Times Guide To Business Networking: How to use the power of your online and offline network to generate career and business success*, Harlow: Financial Times Prentice Hall, Ch. 6

WEBSITES

- Joined Up Networking **www.joinedupnetworking. com/category/on-line-networking-2/ blogging-resources-for-networkers**
- Valuable Content **www.valuablecontent.co.uk**
- Watertight Marketing **www.watertightmarketing.com**
- Problogger **www.problogger.net**

How to build your visibility and profile to generate high-quality, warm leads

In Part 2 of the book we considered how to create a strong brand on which to build your practice. Once you have got all the elements of your brand in place, it's time to work out what you will actually do daily, weekly, monthly and quarterly, to create a predictable pipeline of high-quality leads. This part of the book shows you how to create this pipeline via the most effective routes to market for professionals:

- referral generation via your network
- publishing a book
- PR or article marketing
- speaking
- running events.

6

Networking your way to success

Topics covered in this chapter.

- Why build your network and community?
- How to build your personal networking strategy.
- How to generate referrals via your network.
- Your networking routine.

Your network is your biggest asset when it comes to becoming the Go-To Expert – it can also be the biggest drain on your time. This chapter will help you save time with your networking, by helping you build a personal networking strategy using a five-step process. Within the chapter we introduce you to ways of systematically generating referrals using the SERVICE framework.

> *"We are living in a knowledge economy in which the first thing to recognise is no single person is smart enough by themselves to be genuinely successful."*

> HAMISH TAYLOR, SHINERGISE PARTNERS LTD

Why build your network and community?

The reason that most professionals in practice are taught to network at the start of their career is that it is *the* most effective way to build awareness, get found and generate opportunities. Sit in a café near your work and tune in to the chatter around you – chances are you'll overhear a conversation that goes something like this:

> *"You are thinking of redoing your website/contacting a recruitment consultant/changing accountants? The person you should be talking to is X."*

Ask anyone who is considered to be the Go-To Expert and they will mention the value of their network in helping them build their reputation, extend their reach and get them recommended. The power of personal recommendation is extremely strong. Most high-value purchases, such as engaging a new supplier, involve an element of risk. It's risk that is why someone will always place more faith and trust in a recommendation, rather than someone unknown to them or their network.

Get your networking right and others will do the job of selling for you, spreading the word about your services, products or skills – your own sales force will be happy to spot opportunities on your behalf, and for free!

> *"Our networking activities led to our profit and turnover doubling every year for the last four years, even through the credit crunch and recession."*
>
> GINA WADSWORTH, PARTNER, CONTACT CONSULTANTS

You could have the best service out there, but if no one knows about it or you, how are you going to be found? That's why it is so important for any aspiring Go-To Expert to develop and maintain a strong network of people who can help spread the word about your products, services or skills.

Networking has always been a highly effective tool. As long as commerce has existed, traders have banded together to protect each other from enemies, to govern the conduct of trade and help each other out. But, in today's global, knowledge-based economy it has really come to the fore. We have far greater choice and access to people than ever before, but less time to spend on finding the right people. This is why people are now using their networks more and more to help them rapidly get to the best solution at the first time of asking. With the rise of online networking via social media, you can now build a far larger and more engaged network more easily and more quickly than ever before.

How to build your personal networking strategy

WHAT DO WE MEAN BY A NETWORKING STRATEGY?

Effective business networking is the process of finding, building and maintaining mutually beneficial relationships. Your networking strategy details how you will achieve your goals via your networking activities.

A clear and concise networking strategy will allow you to make the decisions as to *what* networking activities you will do, i.e. it is your *plan* for connecting to important people. If you implement your plan, you will achieve your networking goals. There are five steps involved in creating your networking strategy.

Step 1   Goals – decide what you want to achieve from your networking activities.

Step 2   Audit – assess the suitability of your current networking activities for helping you achieve your networking goals.

Step 3   Find – identify people to add in to your network.

Step 4   Build – progress and deepen the right relationships.

Step 5   Maintain – keep your relationships strong and working for you.

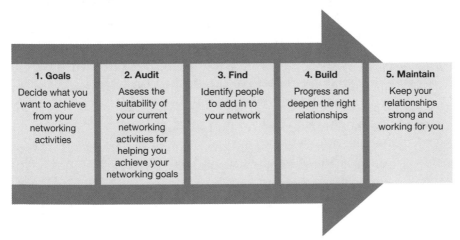

Figure 6.1 The five steps to building your own personal networking strategy

If you complete each stage, your networking plan will almost write itself.

Step 1: Goals

Begin by reviewing your overall business goals because, from those, you can identify the networking goals that will help you achieve the business goals.

Ask yourself, 'What do I really want to achieve via my network?' If you don't have this big goal clear in your mind, it's going to make it very difficult to ensure your networking activities actually happen, because you won't have sufficient motivation to do any or some of these things:

- make the effort to go onto LinkedIn regularly and join in the conversation
- go onto Twitter daily
- head out to a networking event after a long, hard day in the office
- pick up the phone and speak to someone you haven't connected with for a while.

Here are some examples of how networking goals can be linked to business goals.

- To build a client portfolio worth £500,000 within two years, I will use my network to generate four new referrals every quarter.
- To establish a new office in Bristol next year, I will build a personal network in that city during this current year. This network will be of potential clients the new office will need and will assist in identifying new (local) recruits.
- My career goal is to move out of sales and into an events management role within 6–18 months' time. This will require me to network with people in that industry and become known.

To summarise, the main reasons that people go networking are to:

- build their support community
- build their profile

- find and win business
- build their knowledge and expertise base.

It's absolutely fine to network for one, some or all of these reasons – just as long as you are clear about your motives and how this helps you.

Case study 1
Rosemary

Rosemary was a freelance trainer who was keen to build up her reputation and profile in her niche of marketing agencies. She gave herself a networking goal to use Twitter to build up relationships with journalists to get coverage in the marketing trade press. As a result of this strategy she has formed strong relationships with five journalists who write regularly in the marketing trade press. Typically, Rosemary will find that she is quoted in an article by one of these journalists every couple of months.

Networking goals exercise

Now that you have your big networking goals identified, it is time to consider the next stage in building your networking strategy: the audit. This is where you review who is already in your network.

Step 2: Audit

Many people think that they have to build a network from scratch. Actually, each of us naturally has our own network – and, for many of us, there will be some great contacts within our current network who will be able to help us achieve our networking goals. For example, Robert was a long-term member of his golf club. It was only after sitting down with a member of the club, David, that he realised David was a senior decisionmaker in a company that he wanted as a client.

Just because you have a network and are networking all the time, doesn't mean to say that you are doing it in an effective manner, i.e. spending time with the right people in the right places. This is why the second stage of building a networking strategy is to do a networking audit. After all, you don't want to change anything that is working.

The best way to do a networking audit is to draw out your network map. Begin by literally mapping out your ideal network. It's an exercise that will really help you to focus on who you want to meet and how these people are going to help you achieve your business and career goals.

Figure 6.2 Example of a networking map

This may sound rather calculating or manipulative. However, it is a tool to help you focus on how you will spend your networking time. Let's be frank here: how many times have you turned up to a networking event without knowing why you were there and whom you would benefit from meeting? Was it a productive use of your time? A network map will help you visualise your networking time. It also has the additional benefit of helping you to prioritise your networking activities, because you now truly understand why you are networking and why it is important to your future career or business health.

 ### Networking map excercise

Very often many professionals, after completing their networking map, realise that their *current* network contains many of the types of people who can actively help them achieve their networking goals.

Once you have completed your networking map it is time to look critically at the effectiveness of your current networking activities. The networking activity effectiveness exercise can help you do this. For example, ask yourself the following kinds of questions.

- What activities are you doing – such as membership of a professional networking group – that are helping you connect with the right types of people, i.e. hubs?
- What activities are you doing that are helping you achieve your career and business goals?
- What activities are not working for you?
- What activities should you start doing right now?

 ### Networking activity effectiveness exercise

Step 3: Find

Heather often tells a story about George Clooney when delivering a keynote or masterclass on effective business networking. The story goes as follows.

"People are always asking me who I want to meet – I guess this is an occupational hazard of writing a book on networking! I always answer, George Clooney. People then wonder why I answer George Clooney? The fact is, my ultimate goal is to become a kept woman. George Clooney represents someone who could shortcut my way to achieving that goal."

Now, everyone has someone who can help shortcut their way to achieving their networking goals. For example, David Kaye, a retail legal specialist, has found that his relationship with Philip Green, the founder of the Arcadia Group, has led to many referrals to clients in the retail sector.

 Finding people exercise

Step 4: Build

Sadly, many professionals' viewpoint of networking is that it is all about the process of finding contacts.

"Don't count your conversations. Make your conversations count!"

ROB BROWN, BESTSELLING AUTHOR OF *HOW TO BUILD YOUR REPUTATION – THE SECRETS OF BECOMING THE 'GO TO' PROFESSIONAL IN A CROWDED MARKETPLACE*

If you pulled open your desk drawer, how many business cards would prompt the thought, I was meant to get back to them?

That's probably the biggest mistake professionals make with their networking activities. They focus too much on *finding* contacts rather than deepening and maintaining the relationships they have that will help them achieve their business goals via their network.

Once you have identified *who* you need to meet, then you need to categorise them. In the *FT Guide to Business Networking*, there is a simple A, B and C system:

A-lister *Someone who is likely to be able to help you achieve your networking goals in the short and medium term.*

B-lister *Someone who is able to help you achieve your networking goals in the medium and long term.*

C-lister *Someone who is unlikely to be able to help you achieve your networking goals in the long term.*

In your networking strategy, you need to decide on what you will do as a result of meeting an A-, B- or C-lister. We recommend that you connect with everyone on LinkedIn and Twitter, even C-listers, as your, or their, circumstances may change.

We recommend that for A-listers you:

- start a relationship plan for them and diarise next steps from the relationship plan
- aim to speak in person to them at least once every three months
- actively find ways to help them, e.g. by sending them articles that they will find useful
- make at least one introduction and/or referral for them every three months
- include them on a list on Twitter that you check every day.

We recommend that for B-listers you:

- add them to a Twitter list that you check regularly
- find something useful to send to them at least every three months
- aim to speak to them in person at least once a year.

The Excedia 5-level relationship model

The aim with your networking activity is to deepen those relationships that matter to you. Most people realise that not everyone is created equal in their network. In fact, the state of your relationship can be described in a 5-level relationship model, which allows you to categorise the state of your relationship. This is shown in Figure 6.3.

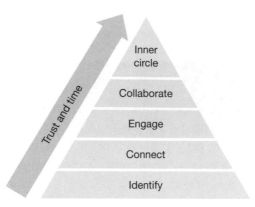

Figure 6.3 The Excedia 5-level relationship model

Level 1: Identify
At this level, you have just become aware of this contact. Maybe someone has mentioned them in conversation or perhaps you have seen a tweet of theirs. Or perhaps they are on an attendance list of an event you are also attending.

Level 2: Connect
At this point you have physically or virtually met a contact and started a one- or two-way conversation, i.e. you have connected. For example, you may have talked to them at a face-to-face networking event or exchanged some tweets or posts within an online forum.

Level 3: Engage
At this point, you have taken a conscious decision to strengthen the relationship and move beyond small talk. This means that you have taken the time to have a one-to-one meeting with them, whether in person or by phone.

Level 4: Collaborate
The trust has built within the relationship to the point where you have agreed to help each other, pass referrals and, potentially, actively look for ways to work together.

Level 5: Inner circle
The relationship is now such that you have worked together and regularly recommend each other's services. There is a strong possibility that

your relationship has developed from a purely professional relationship into a personal friendship.

Case study 2
Tony

Tony was an ambitious surveyor in a large engineering consultancy. He was keen to grow his client portfolio to advance his career within this firm. He noticed the firm was becoming increasingly successful in renewable energy projects. As a result, he actively built his network and key contacts around people, both inside and outside of his firm, with an interest or a specialism in renewable energy. Over a few years his investment in these relationships really started to pay off, as through these relationships he was regularly bringing in new business opportunities for the firm as a whole.

Case study 3
David Kaye

David is known throughout the retail world as the Go-To Expert for legal matters. His relationship with key contacts in the retail world, which included Sir Philip Green whose CEO, Ian Grabiner, was responsible for the growth of his practice and client base. Along the way, his small, niche firm Clairmonts, with a team of 15, worked with many retailing household names, such as Arcadia, Birthdays (Clinton Cards), Reality, a division of GUS (Great Universal Stores), Sports Division (which acquired Olympus), Gadget Shop, USC, d2, MJM Internationalt/aUltimo Lingerie and many others.

Relationship plans

You want to have in place a relationship plan for all your A-listers and potentially some of your B-listers. A relationship plan:

- details what you know about the person and what more you want to know about them
- contains the desired level of contact you want
- indicates what you would like to achieve because of your relationship.

 ## Relationship plan exercise

It's all very well having relationship plans for the folks who matter to you. However, you need to implement these plans. Every month, review all of your relationship plans and check that you have three months of the right level of contact planned into your diary. Then, extend your relationship plans by another month.

> **Tip**
>
> If you have admin assistance available, use it to book in the planned meetings and events that you will attend.

 ## Deepening A-lister relationships exercise

Step 5: Maintain

Think back to your friends at school. How many of them are you still in contact with? Now, those you have lost contact with, do you feel able to pick up the phone and speak with them? I'm guessing not. So, what has made the difference between them and your friends from school who you feel able to still pick up the phone and talk to?

NAME	John Brown	LINKEDIN & TWITTER	www.linkedin.com/in/johncbrown @jcbrown
PHONE	01234 567 8910	WEBSITE	www.johnbrownLLP.co.uk
EMAIL	jcbrown@johnbrownLLP.co.uk	ADDRESS	Business House, 100, Any Street, New Town, AB10 9CD
ROLE	Owner	COMPANY	John Brown LLP
FREQUENCY OF CONTACT			In person: every 6 months, phone call: quarterly, email monthly, Twitter account monitored daily
CURRENT & DESIRED RELATIONSHIP LEVEL (out of 5)			Current – 3, desired – 4
THEIR GOALS & OBJECTIVES			Double the size of their revenue and maintain profit margin in next 2 years Identify 2 assistant solicitors to delegate down to
THEIR INTERESTS OUTSIDE OF WORK			Golf, fine dining, Spurs supporter
FAMILY SITUATION			Married with 2 teenage children, Stephen (13), Alex (15)
HOW CAN I HELP THEM?			Reduce tax bill and start to provide management accounts quarterly
WHAT CONTENT DO THEY WELCOME ME SENDING THEM?			Our monthly newsletter and articles that they may find interesting
RELATIONSHIP NEXT STEPS			Organise next lunch and suggest a round of golf

Figure 6.4 An example of a relationship plan

Yes, regular communication. Without regular communication, your relationships will slip back and lose their usefulness. Therefore, a key part of your networking strategy needs to be how you will keep in touch with your network.

One of the best ways of keeping in touch with the important people in your network is by sending them and sharing with them valuable content. This could be articles or recordings made by you or others.

Tip

Subscribe to the newsletters of people you want to stay close to.

Go back to Chapter 5 and revisit your content plan and, if necessary, change it to identify what content you will share regularly with your A-listers and by what channel you will do this.

How to generate referrals via your network

Having a network is one thing, but using it to build a predictable marketing machine is quite another thing. Your personal networking strategy will get you talking to and in front of the right people, but, if you don't say the right things, then you will miss out on opportunities to generate referrals via your network.

The SERVICE framework will help you use your networking activities to maximise the number of referrals you get through your network. SERVICE stands for:

- Specific
- Extraordinary client service
- Relationships
- Visibility

- Initiative
- Collaborate
- Educate.

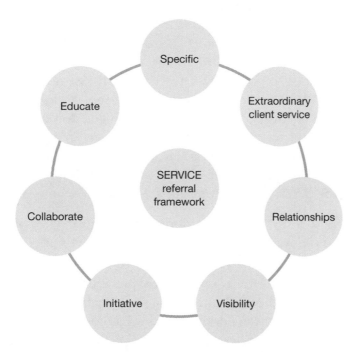

Figure 6.5 The Excedia SERVICE referral framework

SPECIFIC

In Chapter 2 you identified your niche. However, to really reap the benefits of having a niche, you will need to commit to it. Therefore, when you are networking, use the sound bite, credibility statements and stories you created in Part 2. These, rather than claiming to be all things to all people, will help you stand out and be memorable to your ideal clients.

Being specific is more than just being committed to your niche. It is also about being specific with your requests about who you want to be introduced to. If you have done your homework in Part 1, and drawn up your network map, you will know exactly who you want to be introduced to and why.

EXTRAORDINARY CLIENT SERVICE

One of the benefits of being the Go-To Expert is the sheer volume of word-of-mouth recommendations you will generate. Indeed, Simone, a project director for the manufacturing sector, finds that every new client comes to her pretty much pre-sold on the basis of multiple personal recommendations. However, you will only get this word-of-mouth business if you deliver to clients not just good service but extraordinary client service; the type of client service that just compels your clients to tell others about it. (Warning, if you don't deliver on the basics of client service, then any attempt to deliver extraordinary client service will be wasted effort.) Luckily, extraordinary client service can easily be delivered fairly cheaply with just a little thought about what will make the difference to your clients. For example, how about:

- keeping a stock of mobile phone rechargers in your office for when clients visit, so that they can charge their phone while they meet with you or your team.
- taking note of your client's dietary preferences, so you can always offer them a hot beverage and something to eat that you know they can eat/drink and will enjoy
- having some umbrellas in the office so you can walk clients out to their cars when it is raining
- sending them birthday cards
- introducing them to one potential client or referrer every six months
- sending them a small gift, relevant to the work you are doing, after your work is completed, e.g., a conveyancing solicitor sending a small food hamper to their clients on completion day.

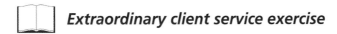 *Extraordinary client service exercise*

RELATIONSHIPS

As already covered, a small core of relationships, i.e. your A-listers, will result in a large proportion of your referrals. When did you last update the relationship plans for your A-listers?

VISIBILITY

Being seen in all the right places, whether online or offline, is a major component for referral generation. For example, Aakar, when he was building his reputation as the Go-To Expert lawyer for the pharmaceutical industry, made sure he was physically present at all the big pharmaceutical trade shows. Your personal networking strategy will make sure that you are networking and being seen in all the right places.

INITIATIVE

One of the best ways of generating referrals is to proactively ask for them, as well as introductions, which may lead to business. However, many of us don't feel we can ask, perhaps because it looks like we are being too pushy. Remember, you are not directly asking for more business from them, just for their help:

> *"I wonder whether you could help me? I'm looking for <insert the type of people you want to meet> who would also benefit from <insert the value you bring>."*

Here are some good opportunities to ask for a referral:

- when a client gives you good feedback
- at the end of an assignment that has gone well
- when the client has recognised that you have gone over and above the call of duty for them.

When clients or people in your network give you referrals or introductions, ask their permission to use their name when making contact. Or even suggest that you could prepare an introduction for them to use via the phone or email.

COLLABORATE

Working together with other professionals who share the same niche market as you can be one of the most powerful ways to generate referrals. Who do you know who has a similar type of client base to you, but offers a different service? In the early days of your relationship you may want to help each other out with little things such as:

- writing blog posts for each other
- quoting them in an article
- recommending them in your newsletters.

As the relationship, trust and credibility builds, it's worth thinking about bigger things you can do together, such as:

- launching a joint service or product
- running a marketing event or campaign together
- systematically introducing all your new clients to them, with an easy incentive to use their services.

 Collaborate exercise

Case study 4
The Franchise Surgery

The Franchise Surgery is a series of surgeries for existing franchisors to come in and speak to professional advisers who specialise in franchising. The surgery was co-founded by Carl Reader, an accountant who specialises in franchising. For each surgery, they tend to get six to ten franchisors. Every professional adviser in attendance normally comes away with invoiceable business from each surgery session.

EDUCATE

If you want your network to act as an unpaid sales force for you, then you will need to educate them as to how to spot a potential client, how much you value them doing this for you and what to do next. Go back to Chapter 3 and look at your sound bite and the pain points you solve for your clients. How can your network physically see, hear, taste or even smell that someone needs your services? What are the sorts of comments that you will hear them make?

For example, someone who may be ready to change their accountant will say things like:

- 'I'm not sure what my accountant actually does to justify what he is charging me.'
- 'My accountant only seems to get in touch with me when he wants his bill paid or year end is on us.'
- 'I'm unhappy with the current level of service I am receiving from my accountant.'
- 'My business is growing rapidly and I think it may be outgrowing my current accountant.'

You also need to educate your network that giving you referrals is a good thing. Do this by saying thank you. You could:

- send them a handwritten note saying thank you
- give them a gift
- give them a referral in return
- buy them lunch or a drink
- offer them a spotter's fee or commission split for any successful introductions or referrals, but be aware that some professionals may not, either for ethical or regulatory reasons, be able to accept a spotter's fee or commission split.

 **Educate exercise**

Your networking routine

In this chapter we have talked about how you are going to network your way to success and started to think about what you are going to do to implement your networking strategy. Using the output from the exercises in this chapter, and your content plan from the previous chapter, go through your notes and identify what you will do daily, weekly and monthly to achieve your networking goals.

DAILY NETWORKING ROUTINE
• Check my 'people to keep close to' list and @mentions on Twitter • Do my 9-minute daily LinkedIn routine
WEEKLY NETWORKING ROUTINE
• Attend fortnightly breakfast meeting • Add new blog post to Defero Law • Check prominent legal bloggers and comment on at least one new blog post • Find 20–30 articles to share on Twitter and LinkedIn for the next week
MONTHLY NETWORKING ROUTINE
• Update my relationship plans and plan activity for next 3 months • Plan my blogging content for the next week

Figure 6.6 Example of a networking routine

 *Networking routine exercise*

Summary

Your network – and how you use your network – is often the easiest way to generate new business. However, to make sure you don't waste time networking, be clear about:

- what the purpose and goal for your networking strategy and its activities are
- who you want to meet and why you want to meet them
- what you will do to deepen A-lister relationships in your network to drive your networking goals (and, ultimately, your business goals)

When you are with your network, you need to be proactive in order to help them pass you referrals. Use the SERVICE framework to help educate them as to what you want and need and how they can help you to do that.

Action points

1 Complete the networking map exercise and identify three action points to add to new relationships where there are gaps.

2 Complete the deepening the A-list relationships exercise. Make sure you add the next steps from your relationship plans into your diary.

3 Revisit your content plan and revise it, based on your work in this chapter.

4 Speak to your best clients and find out where to spend time both physically and online. Go and meet two potential new A-listers this month.

Further resources

For help building your networking strategy and generating more business through the relationships in your network, we recommend these resources.

BOOKS

- Ferrazzi, K. (2005) *Never Eat Alone: And other secrets to success, one relationship at a time*, New York, NY: Doubleday Business
- Lopata, A. (2011) *Recommended: How to sell through networking and referrals*, Harlow: Financial Times
- Misner, I. R. (2008) *29% Solution: 52 weekly networking success stories*, Austin, TX: Greenleaf Book Group
- Townsend, H. (2011) *The Financial Times Guide To Business Networking: how to use the power of your online and offline network to generate career and business success*, Harlow: Financial Times Prentice Hall

WEBSITES

- Joined Up Networking **www.joinedupnetworking.com**
- Business Networking **www.business-networking.co.uk**
- Relationology – the art and science of creating relationships – **www.relationology.co.uk**
- Global Networking Council – interviews with the top worldwide networking experts – **www.globalnetworkingcouncil.com**

7

Publishing your way to success

Topics covered in this chapter.

- The benefits of writing a business book.
- The challenges of writing a business book.
- The five steps to writing and successfully marketing your book.
- How to decide whether to go published or self-published.

Becoming an author conveys a level of credibility and expertise that sometimes can singlehandedly give you the status and kudos of the Go-To Expert. Your own business book is often called a 'business card on steroids' and used to be an essential requirement for any highly paid professional speaker. Historically, if you wanted to be seen as the Go-To Expert, having a book to your name was vital. In the current climate, that is not always the case, although having 'published author' on your CV is incredibly valuable.

Writing a book is a massive time commitment and one that many professionals don't feel able to give. This chapter will give you the knowledge you need regarding what is involved in writing and marketing a book, so you can decide if this is something you want to commit to.

> *"It's mechanically very simple to assemble a book but somehow your fame, your respect goes up considerably if you have a book to your name."*
>
> CHARLES H. GREEN, CO-AUTHOR OF *THE TRUSTED ADVISOR* AND AUTHOR OF *TRUST-BASED SELLING: USING CUSTOMER FOCUS AND COLLABORATION TO BUILD LONG-TERM RELATIONSHIPS*

The benefits of writing a business book

The benefits of writing a business book are many, so that's why so many professionals want to write a book. The title of *published author* also confers with it status and authority. Which professional wouldn't want this? In addition, the credibility of writing a book often allows you the option to increase your charge-out rates.

> *"My book has helped me to explain why my subject matters and has therefore supported me in building strong commercial partnerships. As a result of writing my book, I've deepened my knowledge of the marketplace, which is enabling me to offer services that my clients really want."*

> SHIREEN SMITH, IP SOLICITOR, AZRIGHTS, AND AUTHOR OF
> *LEGALLY BRANDED*

A business book, both in the writing of it and the publishing of it, can open doors. For example, many often-hard-to-reach decisionmakers will make time to be interviewed for a book. Conference organisers will often deliberately target newly published authors, partly because they think they can get them to appear for free or at a vastly reduced rate, but, also, they are perceived to have something new and fresh to say.

One of the benefits of writing a business book, which isn't always acknowledged, is it forces you to marshal your thoughts, so your IP

Case study 1
Legally Branded

Shireen Smith had been trying to write a book to help grow her business for over a year and had managed to write just two chapters, as she found it difficult to devote the necessary time. After she joined a programme, she learned how to plan the book, and discovered the importance of focusing on the book as the single most important project to get it written. She worked closely with an editor and used to write every morning for over six months. Still, it took quite a few first drafts to finalise the book and, in the end, it took over two years for the book to get written. However, it was worth the effort as, nine months after publishing the book, her business revenue tripled as a result. In her words, writing *Legally Branded* was the hardest thing she has ever done.

crystallises in your mind. There is nothing like writing about a subject to clarify exactly what you mean and how you actually utilise your skill for a client. This process of firming up your knowledge normally makes you better at what you do.

Finally, some professionals have always wanted a write a book. They have had 'write a book' on their professional 'bucket list' for many years. After all, the respect you get, because you have written a book, from your peers, friends and family is certainly worth having. The satisfaction of finally getting your name in print on a physical book can, if some professionals are honest, be their prime motivation for writing a business book.

The challenges of writing a business book

Whilst the business benefits of writing a book are undeniably attractive, there are many challenges and downsides to writing a business book, too. Let's be brutally honest, writing a book will not bring you fame and fortune directly. Most published business book writers will make only between 50p and £1.50 a book in royalties. This is not a lot when you consider how many copies of business books actually sell – 98 per cent of business books will sell fewer than 500 copies. As a rule of thumb, any published business book that sells over 8,000 copies, and any self-published book that sells over 800 copies, is considered to be a business book bestseller. The *FT Guide to Business Networking*, which sold over 5,000 copies in its first year, was in the Top 150 business books sold in the UK that year. In other words, don't give up the day job after publishing your first business book!

As a rule of thumb, writing a business book will consume your focus for at least 12 months. This could be less for a self-published short e-book, but, ultimately, good writing takes time to produce. Whilst you may be great at writing short and crisp 500-word blog articles, scaling this up to a 60,000-word book is another matter entirely. (We both know that from painful experience!) To write and market a business book successfully you will need to focus approximately a day a week for 12 months. Not all professionals – particularly those employed within a practice – have the time to dedicate to writing.

From our collective experiences of writing a book, it can be incredibly tough going at times. Perhaps the greatest personal challenge is when an author's beautifully crafted first draft comes back from the editor with entire paragraphs brutally crossed out with red pen. A comment like 'Too negative' can really bruise a professional's ego and this is why so many brilliant people never finish their books.

The five steps to writing and successfully marketing your book

Many first-time authors think the first step to becoming an author is to write the manuscript. This is actually the last step in the process. Failure to complete the first four steps could, from painful past experiences, result in many hours of writing being wasted.

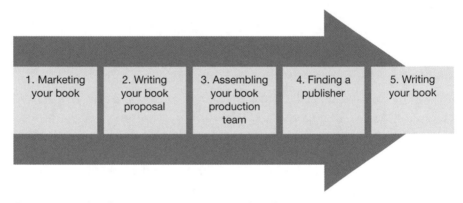

Figure 7.1 The five steps to writing a book

1 MARKETING YOUR BOOK

Ideally you will start to market your book at the point you decide to write it. The more time you have to warm up your community, friends and family and get them gasping to read your book, the more copies you will shift. The marketing of your book will run in parallel to the writing of your book and carry on way after your book has been published.

2 WRITING YOUR BOOK PROPOSAL

Your book proposal is a formal statement of your aim in writing a book. Within the proposal you demonstrate your commitment to writing the book by putting together a comprehensive plan. You may hear this document being called a *pitch*. This document is essential, whether you plan to publish or self-publish, as it is the equivalent of an architect's plan for a new house.

Typically, a book proposal will contain the following ten components:

1 the personal and professional 'why' for your book
2 the market positioning for your book
3 the three-sentence elevator pitch
4 your book's title and subtitle
5 a description of your book
6 a pen portrait of your book's readers and how your book will help them
7 what aspects of your book will help it to be successful
8 your book's content, including detailed individual chapter plans
9 information about the author
10 your author platform, or, how you plan to market the book.

The personal and professional 'why' for your book

What's your motivation for writing a book? Are you just looking to produce a slim e-book to use as an incentive for people to sign up on your website or do you want a beautifully produced printed book that showcases your credibility and expertise? Your motivation for wanting to write a book will give you direction on these choices and the time you want to devote to the project.

The market positioning for your book

It is very rare for a book to be published that focuses on a completely original idea or topic. Most newly published (or self-published books) either take an established topic and put the author's spin on it or extend current thinking in a certain area. Being a first mover for a new topic or thought can be a blessing or a curse. For example, you may find that no one has written a book on the subject you are proposing because there is minimal or no demand for that topic.

Your aim when thinking about your book is to answer the question, 'What's going to be different about my book?'

The three-sentence elevator pitch

Your pitch helps you crystallise the reason why people will want to read your book. Ideally, this needs to be about 3 sentences and 50 words. Whilst this may seem like an unnecessary exercise, it is vital to help you, the author, be very clear and focused on what you are writing.

Example of a three-sentence elevator pitch

The FT Guide to Business Networking: *This book teaches the networking skills that today's time-pressed professionals need to get on in business. It tells you all you need to know about the art of building contacts effectively face-to-face and online through social networking: this online/offline combination and focus on the specific needs of professionals sets it apart from any other book on business networking.*

Your book's title and subtitle

Typically a book tends to have a short one- to three-word title, then a subtitle that is a longer sentence describing the benefit that the readers can expect if they read the book. For example:

- *Valuable Content Marketing: How to Make Quality Content the Key to Your Business Success*
- *Principled Selling: How to Win More Business Without Selling Your Soul*
- *Double Your Business: How to Break Through the Barriers to Higher Growth, Turnover and Profit.*

A catchy title with a strong promise to the reader is vital for your book's success, because a good title will make a potential publisher want to read your book's proposal and help sell your book instantly to the reader.

Don't worry if you know you will struggle to pick a good book title. Your publisher may help you with your title or a brainstorm with friends may unlock a wealth of good ideas.

A description of your book

This is where you describe your book's purpose and approach. This will cover:

- what your book sets out to do for the reader
- why it will be interesting or compelling for the reader
- what you have to say that will be original
- what important problem or question your book provides the answer to and why this is important to your reader
- the need for your book
- what the reader will learn
- the gap in the market for this book.

A pen portrait of your book's readers and how your book will help them

This is where you consider who the readers for your book are.

- Who will buy your book?
- Describe the target readership for your book.
- How will this book be of value to your readership?

You may find the work you did in Chapter 3 of this book, particularly the pain points, useful when thinking about how this book will help your readership.

What aspects of your book will help it to be successful

This is where you start to think about the content and style of the book you want to write.

- How will you structure your book?
- In what practical ways will this book help readers to achieve something good?

- What are the most compelling contributions that your book will make in this market? Highlight the ideas, insights, research, frameworks, tools or techniques that will be most interesting to your audience.
- What are the most resonant cases, stories or examples in your book?

Your book's content, including detailed individual chapter plans

A detailed individual chapter plan for your book will save you many hours of editing, thinking and rewriting time. Your chapter plan provides structure and a route map for your writing.

Your aim when thinking about your content is to:

- list all the chapters of the book and, in bullet points or a few sentences, describe the contents of each one
- decide on whether you divide your book up into parts or sections
- consider whether you need an introduction, overview and/or final chapter summary.

Information about the author

This is where you present your credentials to write this book. Whether or not you intend to self-publish or publish, this is a useful exercise to do. Your thoughts for this part of your proposal will be useful for the book jacket and 'About the author' sections of the book.

Your author platform, or, how you plan to market the book

This is where you think about the marketing plan for your book. Whether or not you self-publish or publish, the person who is most likely to drive sales (or demand for copies of your book) will be you and other people in your firm. A commercial publisher will expect to see a detailed marketing plan here and the stronger your author platform, the more likely they will be to commission your book.

A well thought-out, thoroughly researched and beautifully written book proposal typically will take you a full week to put together, write, edit and polish. At times it can feel very hard just writing your proposal. The best way to view this part of the process positively is as a necessary evil, which is toughening you up to actually write the book!

3 ASSEMBLING YOUR BOOK PRODUCTION TEAM

A business book is something that you rarely write by yourself or in isolation. As an author, it is easy to get completely immersed in your 'baby', so it becomes very difficult to stand back and critically evaluate your writing.

Here are some of the people you will need to gather around you to help get the book out of your head and into the published form.

Book project manager

This person will manage the process of producing your book, right from idea conception through to marketing the finished article. If your book is being published, your publisher will provide a book project manager to take your signed-off manuscript through to the final printed book.

Literary agent

Agents help their clients identify editors and also craft book proposals. They will also pitch your book to an editor on your behalf. Typically, agents will want 20 per cent of the book's royalties. This is the reason why most non-fiction authors do not use an agent, as the book's royalties are not high enough to warrant the use of an agent's time and expertise.

Commissioning editor

This is the person at the publishing company who commissions authors to write books. As well as finding authors to write the books on his or her 'list', the editor will generally take on the book project manager role and project editor role for any books on his or her list. It is not uncommon for a commissioning editor to be handling 50 books on his or her list.

Editor

Your editor will take your words and, if the editor is good, turn them into something where the words zing off the page and the message you wanted to communicate shines through. Whether or not you plan to publish or self-publish, you will need to hire your own editor. Most publishers' ideal is to receive a manuscript that only needs a minimal edit.

The words in your head that you present to a live audience, for example as part of a training session, will not work when you commit them to paper for readers who are not even in the same city as you. Therefore, your words need to work first time for this invisible audience. Your words have to hold their hands, guiding and encouraging their progress through the chapters, augmented by careful use of examples/case studies, all of which work in your absence. A good editor will help you make the transition from 'expert' to 'writer', all the while maintaining the integrity of your expertise in your special subject.

Book reviewers

Your book reviewers split into two camps: those who sense-check your writing as you write it and those who write a positive review about your book, which may be used on your book jacket and marketing materials. Ideally you want the reviews on the book jacket to come from people who have credibility within your niche market.

Copy editor

This person will edit your text, checking for grammatical and other errors and that all the references, citations and signposts to content within your manuscript are correct. The editor will also check that you have the relevant permission for any quotes used within the book. If you decide to use a publisher, they will provide you with a copy editor.

Typesetter

This is the person who will take your manuscript and typeset it so that it is in a format that can be given to a printer to print. If you decide to use a publisher, they will choose a template for the book and arrange to typeset the book for you.

Proofreader

This person will proofread your typeset manuscript to pick up any typos or obvious mistakes. Typically, at least two people, as well as you, will do the proofreading. If you go down the published route, your publisher typically will employ professional proofreaders.

Indexer, illustrator and cover designer

Your indexer and cover designer will produce an index and cover design for your book and, normally, will be supplied by your publisher. Your illustrator will redraw any illustrations, diagrams and pictures you provide for your book and, normally, will not be supplied by your publisher.

4 FINDING A PUBLISHER

If you decide to go for the publisher route, once you have written your proposal, it is time to find a publisher. Most publishers will reject over 95 per cent of all the proposals that they receive.

Here are our tips to get your proposal document read and accepted.

- Get introduced to a commissioning editor at a publishing company by one of their existing authors. This will increase the probability that your proposal will get read quickly.
- Do not harass a commissioning editor about your proposal after you have sent it to them. Let them come back to you – they will if they like the proposal.
- Only approach publishers that specialise in the type of book you want to write. Most publishers' websites will have a section for authors stating what sort of books they are likely to commission.
- You may be able to find the email addresses of the publishers' commissioning editors on the publishers' websites.
- Download from the publishers' websites the proposal templates that the publishers typically use. Use these templates for your proposals.
- Remember that many commissioning editors will have a limit on their 'list' – i.e. the number of books that they are handling at any one time. If their list is full for the year, even if you are likely to write the next *7 Effective Habits*, they still wouldn't commission you.

- Most commissioning editors for non-fiction books would expect to deal directly with the author rather than a literary agent.
- Spend over 25 per cent of your time building the commercial case for your book in your proposal. Remember that your publisher wants to make money from your book, not help you get your name in print.

Getting a publisher to approach you to write a book

Make no mistake, getting your book commissioned and published is a tough ask. However, as Lee Duncan found with his book *Double Your Business* and Catrin Mills with *Making Every 6 Minutes Count*, every now and then a publisher will approach a Go-To Expert and see if they are interested in writing a book for them. This tends to happen when the following conditions are true: the publisher has in mind a book it wants for its list and the author is active on social media and regularly writing about their 'thing'.

An active blogger with a highly engaged readership is often a prime target for a commissioning editor. Whether or not you approach the publisher, or they approach you, you will still need to write a strong proposal with a clear commercial benefit to the publisher before they will commission your book.

5 WRITING YOUR BOOK

If you have taken the time with your book proposal to build detailed content plans for each chapter, then writing your book becomes much easier. Your aim when writing is to write it only once and minimise any rewrites or lengthy edits.

Tip

Whilst it may be tempting to use Pages or Open Office to write your manuscript, you will save much heartache and many formatting problems by writing your manuscript in Microsoft Word. This is the publishing industry's standard word processor.

When you decide to write a book on top of your day job and family commitments, ratcheting up the word count can take its toll on the people around you and you personally. Here are some tips from real authors to help you get the writing done.

- Work with a good editor. An editor brings a critical eye to the whole process and, unlike an author, who often can't see the wood for the trees – won't get caught up in the small details. The editor will advise you on both the minutiae as well as the big structural stuff.

- Working with a co-author helps to share the burden of writing, but not as much as you think it might. The time you save in the words you need to write is often balanced out by the extra time required to work together, critique each other's writing and try to seamlessly knit all the bits you are writing together. Typically more time will be needed in the editing process if you work with a co-author. A detailed chapter and content plan is essential if you intend to write with someone else!

- Find a time when the words flow. Everyone finds that they have more productive times for them personally to write. Sharon Tanton, co-author of *Valuable Content Marketing*, found herself getting up at 06:30 a.m. for weeks to get her book written; her co-author, Sonja Jefferson, found it easier to write in the evening.

- Overestimate how long it will take to write the book and pick a date when you want to have finished the last word in the last chapter. Then add another month into your writing schedule to allow for emergencies, holidays, writer's block and client demands. Expect that the first 25 per cent of the book will take 50 per cent of your time to write.

- If you struggle to write words, always remember that you cannot edit a blank sheet. Getting *any* words down gives you some basis for improvement.

- Create deadlines for yourself. It doesn't matter whether these are real deadlines or not, but they help to focus the mind and the writing effort. A publisher will give you a deadline. If you are self-publishing, work with someone to help keep you to your planned publication date.

- Take time out from the day job to get big chunks of the book written. A large portion of this book was written when Heather had taken two weeks off over the school Easter holidays. Those two weeks contributed to at least half the book being written.

- Reward yourself when you complete each chapter. It's amazing how much more focused you can be if you have a personally motivating reward waiting for you when you get to a milestone.

- Record and transcribe the interviews you do as part of your research for your book. This gives you a permanent record of your conversation and using a transcription makes it much easier to find pithy appropriate quotes to use throughout the book. It also frees you up from note-taking during the interview so you can concentrate on what is being said.

- Just do it. It's amazing how much procrastinating you can do when you *should* be writing your book. Give yourself a daily or weekly word count target. Then make sure you achieve your word counts before you can do some of the nice things you have planned. The hardest paragraph to write is the first paragraph. Once you've done this paragraph it gets easier. Block out two four-hour chunks in your diary to write your first chapter.

- Don't get too hung up on writing exactly what you envisaged you would write in your content plan for the book. As you research and write the book, it will take shape as it goes along. This is normal and you may need to adjust the chapter structure and contents as you go.

- Raise the commitment stakes by telling people you are actually going to write your book. It's amazing what the shame of not writing your book will actually prompt you to do. Although writing your book may take you away from paid work, writing is still valid work from which you plan to get a future benefit.

Tip

If writing is really not your thing or you are struggling with writer's block, write your book using a series of interviews. Write out a series of questions that will help you produce the content for a chapter. Use an audio typist to get a transcription of the interview. Your interview transcription will give you a huge amount of editable content for your book.

How to decide whether to go published or self-published

One of the big decisions you will need to take fairly early on in your journey is whether to go for a publishing deal or to self-publish your book. There are advantages and disadvantages to both routes. The decision to publish or self-publish is never straightforward and will really depend on your personal circumstances.

TRADITIONAL PUBLISHING

ADVANTAGES	DISADVANTAGES
The publisher and their team know what they are doing. Consequently they will guide you through the book production process.	A typical publisher will take between four and nine months to produce your book and get it on to the shelves.
The publisher takes all the initial risk and cost of getting the book into print. They will pay for printing, design, delivery and project management of the book production process.	When you sign a contract with a publishing house you are signing away some of your ownership rights.
You may get given £1–3,000 as an advance for a first-time author.	It is fairly typical to expect royalties equating to 10 per cent of net returns. Depending on your book's retail price this may not be a lot.
The publisher is able to get your book through the traditional channels into more national and international bookstores and wholesalers than you can alone.	Many authors wrongfully believe, if they get their book published, they will also get the backing of a publisher's huge marketing machine. That machine is often pitifully small and stretched across many titles.
Being published by some of the big traditional publishers such as the *Financial Times* still confers kudos and credibility that a self-published book will struggle to emulate.	Your publisher controls your book. This could mean that they may want to change the title of your book and even what you actually write about and who you write it for.

▶

ADVANTAGES	DISADVANTAGES
Your publisher will be keen to get the book on to the shelves and start to realise money from their investment in you. Consequently, you will get set a deadline by your publisher. This deadline will be incredibly motivating.	Most publishers are not set up to deal with the requirements of a niche market. They will want to commission a book that has a large and broad market appeal. Typically, they will want you to prove in your book proposal that they will easily be able to sell over 2,000 copies of your book.
Very often there is a marked difference in the written and printed quality between a self-published and published book. Self-published books are often seen as being of poor quality.	
They handle all of the printing, distribution and order fulfilment side of the bookselling.	

SELF-PUBLISHING

ADVANTAGES	DISADVANTAGES
It's truly your book. You choose the style, the audience, the title, the look, the feel and the cover design.	Once you have written your book, you will still need to edit, design the layout, proofread and typeset the book, then find a cover designer, printer and someone to store your books. Finding and managing this team takes time. Time that you may not have on top of your day job.
Depending on your standards for the finish and quality of the writing, you can have your book up on an e-book stall within days of you finishing the last word.	It's tough to write and produce a bad book and it's even tougher to write and produce a high-quality good book. Knowing all the steps in the process to get a book out at the other end takes energy.
As it is your book, you (or your firm!) get to keep all the monies you make from book sales. Remember that you will need to factor in printing, storage and fulfilment costs for every book you sell. However, depending on your price point, there is no reason why you can't make upwards of £5 per copy sold.	If you want your book to come across as a quality book, both in terms of the writing and the look and feel of the book, this will cost you money up front. Expect to spend at least £3,000 to write and produce a high-quality printed version of your book.

▶

ADVANTAGES	DISADVANTAGES
It is cheaper to provide copies of books for clients and prospects. Most publishers will give their own authors only a 50 per cent discount on the book's recommended retail price.	
Many middlemen are now around to help you do the heavy lifting. For example, companies like CreateSpace will provide an extremely cost-effective print on demand solution for you, so that you don't need to worry about printing, fulfilment or distribution.	

HEALTH WARNING

It can be very tempting to take shortcuts to get your book quickly and cheaply produced. We would caution against this. After all, if you are going to devote time and money to writing and producing a book, you owe it to yourself to create the right and best book you can. A poorly written, structured or edited book may damage your reputation rather than enhance it.

Summary

A business book is often said to be the best business card you can buy. Authors of business books tend to command respect and credibility. Plus, by writing a book, you may shortcut the process of becoming the Go-To Expert. Historically, if you wanted to be a highly paid professional speaker, you needed a book to your name before you could hit the big time.

There are five steps to writing your book:

1 marketing your book
2 writing your book proposal
3 assembling your book production team
4 finding a publisher
5 writing your book.

Action points

1   Talk to other published authors about their experiences in writing a book. Write down their best advice and ask them for the pitfalls to avoid. Ask to see a copy of their book proposal.

2   If you are employed in a firm, talk with key decisionmakers to see if they will support you with time and resources to write a book.

3   Look at your business bookshelf. Ask yourself, what distinguishes the best books from the rest? What do the writers and publishers of these books do well?

4   Decide on whether or not you will write a business book. If you decide to write a book:

   a. download a blank book proposal form from **www.joinedupnetworking.com**

   b. fill out your book proposal

   c. buy key competitors' books and read them, taking notes of strengths and weaknesses.

Further resources

For help to write, publish and market your book, we recommend the following resources and suppliers.

BOOKS

- Bowerman, P. (2006) *The Well-Fed Self Publisher: How to turn one book into a full-time living*, Atlanta, GA: Fanove Publishing
- Kawasaki, G. and Welch, C. (2013) *APE: Author, Publisher, Entrepreneur: How to write and publish a book*, USA: Nononina Press

WEBSITES

- Valuable Content **www.valuablecontent.co.uk**
- Sue Richardson Associates **www.suerichardson.co.uk**

8

Speaking your way to success

Topics covered in this chapter.

- Why you need to add speaking to your marketing mix.
- The difference between 'public speaking' and 'presenting'.
- How to design a speech that helps you achieve your objectives.
- How to deliver a speech with impact.
- How to conquer your nerves.
- What should be included in your speaker kit.
- How to successfully secure speaking engagements.

The traditional route to achieving the Go-To Expert status was to write a book and then, off the back of the book, speak at conferences and events. However, public speaking is often feared and many professionals would prefer to have their teeth taken out without anaesthetic, than give a presentation, let alone a keynote speech to open up a conference. This chapter will help equip you with the ability to secure speaking engagements and deliver an energising and compelling keynote speech.

> *"To spread your message you have to speak."*
>
> SHIREEN SMITH, IP SOLICITOR, AZRIGHTS, AND AUTHOR OF
> *LEGALLY BRANDED*

Why you need to add speaking to your marketing mix

Public speaking, or presenting for that matter, is normally not on most professionals 'must do' list. After all, there is nothing quite so nerve-wracking as standing up in front of a few hundred people. However, we believe that, if you do add speaking into your marketing mix, you will gain these advantages:

- the chance to speak to lots of decisionmakers and buyers of your services in the same place at the same time
- potentially, a very high appearance fee – e.g. a very good professional speaker, at the top of their game, can command fees of over £5,000 + expenses per speaking engagement
- a conference organiser building your profile for you, by using your details and credentials to help publicise their event
- the chance to network with other speakers at an event
- the opportunity to be paid to attend a conference where your niche market hangs out
- promotional opportunities to sell your books and services, either from the stage or afterwards when networking with audience members.

The difference between 'public speaking' and 'presenting'

There is a subtle difference between *public speaking* and *presenting*. The difference is how the skills are utilised. If you are giving a speech, typically you would expect to deliver this standing in front of your audience who will listen to you without interruption – unless you invite questions or discussions from the floor. In fact, many speakers are seen as part motivators, part informers and part entertainers. Good public speakers will not use any notes, very often get their point across using the medium of storytelling and may or may not use a mix of visuals (music, video, pictures) to enhance their message.

Contrast this with a typical presentation. Very often a presentation will be delivered in a less formal environment, to either a small or large room full of colleagues, clients or prospects. Normally the presenter will support their delivery with visual aids, e.g. diagrams, handouts, bullet-pointed slides. When presenting, you may be sitting down or standing up in front of the room.

At a simple level, a speaker will be asked to deliver a keynote, whilst a presenter will be asked to present on a topic. A keynote is normally 45 minutes in length, but can be extended or shortened, depending on the requirements of the event organiser.

THE TWO DIFFERENT TYPES OF SPEAKERS

Speakers are often referred to as 'content' speakers or 'motivational' speakers.

> *Content speakers* will often talk to the audience about their specialist subject. For example, Tim Luscombe is known as the corporate finance speaker.

> *Motivational speakers* will use some aspect of the story of their life to inspire their audience. For example, Rory MacKenzie, a military amputee, uses his experience of being injured whilst serving with the British Army and going on to row the Atlantic, to get across two key points to his audience: success is a decision and motivation is optional.

How to design a speech that helps you achieve your objectives

The corporate world seems to believe that the first stage in delivering a speech is to reach for the PowerPoint slides. *No, no, no!* This, if you are going to use slides at all, should be the last part of the design process. If you follow this nine-step process when designing your speech, then you will almost always, on paper, have a keynote that will help you achieve your objectives.

STEP 1: DECIDE ON WHAT YOU WANT TO ACHIEVE IN YOUR SPEECH

There is a reason you have been asked to deliver this speech. The person who booked you to speak, your booker, will be able to tell you what they want to achieve as a result of your speaking at their event. Is it to inform, persuade, sell, inspire, request action? What is it? You may find that your booker already has a title in mind for your slot on the programme.

STEP 2: DO YOUR AUDIENCE ANALYSIS

Now that you know your objective for the speech, it is time to research what you know about the audience – and what your booker can tell you about the audience.

- What do you know about your audience?
- Who are the main decisionmakers?
- What will make your audience sit up and listen?
- What has your audience been promised for the speech?
- How does your audience like to take in information?
- What style of speaking does your audience like?
- What will the other speakers be talking about?

You will select your content and the flow of the speech based on the answers to these questions.

STEP 3: DECIDE ON A MAXIMUM OF THREE MAIN PIECES OF CONTENT

The best speakers use the medium of storytelling to communicate their message. The reason is that stories help to engage the audience at a deeper level, as well as improving recall. Typically, they will use a structure like this with each story:

- tell the story
- draw out the point from the story
- give a relevant example
- invite the audience to take action.

You may be thinking, why a maximum of three main pieces of content? It has been proven by research[3] that humans are programmed to remember effectively up to three or, at most, four things. Add in more ideas or content and you will find that your audience will forget more of the speech or your arguments and so the reasons to take actions will start to suffer from argument dilution.

[3] Wiseman, R. (2010) *59 Seconds: Think a Little, Change a Lot*, London: Pan Macmillan.

Your aim when designing your keynote is to weave your content so each story moves on seamlessly and in a logical fashion to the next story. The more thinking time your audience is using up trying to work out why you've just started talking about something, the less time they are thinking about what you are actually saying.

Very often you will be asked to deliver a speech that will be expected to last more than 20 minutes. To help keep the audience's concentration high throughout the entire duration of the presentation you may need to change the speech's dynamics, such as adding in:

- a question and answer session
- an interactive exercise for the audience to complete
- a video clip.

Tip

Occasionally you find yourself having the privilege of addressing a conference in your role as the conference sponsor. In our experience, this is normally the cue for delegates to switch off. If you are in this position, our advice is to keep your presentation short and sweet, practise it, ditch your slides and resist the opportunity to 'sell' to delegates. In your slot, aim to tell a couple of stories that illustrate the benefits of working with you and offer delegates a piece of valuable content if they come to see you.

STEP 4: WRITE YOUR OPENING

How you open your speech will determine how well your time on the stage will be received. It is in the first minute that your audience will decide on how much attention to pay to you.

To start your speech off on the right foot, request that the event host introduces you to the audience. Do script this introduction for your event host, using it to establish your credentials with the audience, and what you will be talking about in your speech. Ideally, your introduction will include a 'hook', which will start to make them think and entice them to listen.

When you start your speech, your first aim is to establish rapport with the audience and earn the right to 'tell your story'. Too much 'I' or 'We' before you have earned the right to tell your story will risk breaking any early rapport you have established with your audience.

These are two main different types of opening.

> **The open loop** *This is where you start your speech with the beginning of a story or by raising a question with the audience. You answer the question or finish the story only at the end of your speech.*

> **The story** *This is where you tell a story that you know will engage the audience and generate rapport with them. Typically, you will want to tell your best story first.*

After you have opened your speech and generated rapport with your audience, then you want to give your audience a preview of what they will gain from your speech.

STEP 5: WRITE YOUR CLOSE

This is the last part of your speech and just as important to get right as the opening part of the speech. Think back to your speech's objective: what do you want the audience to do as a result of this speech? What actions can you ask them to do, to help you achieve your speech's objective? These need to go into your close. As much as possible you want to link the end of your speech to the beginning of your speech and end your speech on a high note. When you are thinking about your close, how can you do something out of the ordinary? Something that will make you memorable? Whilst you may not be able to finish with a song (and a high E) like Celia Delaney did at the Professional Speaker Association's spring convention in 2013, do make sure you end on a metaphorical high note. Do plan exactly what you will say in your ending and commit to it 100 per cent.

As well as the action you want your audience to take, your close needs to include:

- a summary of the main points of the speech and how these help the audience achieve the 'hook' you started with in the opening section of your speech
- an opportunity for the audience to ask questions.

STEP 6: WRITE YOUR TRANSITIONS

The transitions in your speech are the short sentences that signpost to your audience where you are in the speech and where you are about to go. These signposts help your audience orientate themselves in the speech, as well as improving their concentration.

Examples of these transitions would include:

- 'Now we've finished examining…, we are going to…'
- 'I've now finished the main part of this keynote and would like to wrap up and conclude…'

STEP 7: DECIDE WHEN AND HOW YOU WANT TO TAKE QUESTIONS

As a rule of thumb, audience's questions need to be encouraged. When the audience asks questions, it is normally a good indicator that they are listening and thinking about what you are saying. However, you, as the speaker, need to direct your audience in how and when you would like questions. There are pros and cons to having questions as you go along or asking for questions to be kept until the end. As a rule of thumb, if your timing is very tight or you are not that confident about delivering your material, ask for questions at the end.

Tip

Always have one question pre-prepared for the event host to kick off question time.

STEP 8: SLIDES OR NO SLIDES?

This is a fairly contentious issue amongst speakers. When you decide not to use slides, you make your audience rely solely on an auditory channel. This can make it difficult for your audience to grasp key concepts, understand the flow of an argument or remember key facts. Therefore slides, used sparingly, can help increase the emotional impact of your words as well as enhance recall and comprehension. As they say, a picture is worth a thousand words. However, do not be tempted to write your notes on a slide. Slides are not there to help you – the speaker – remember your words! If you write your notes on a slide, you will hinder recall and comprehension because most people struggle to cope with two pieces of language at the same time.

Good slides will:

- include pictures that inform and entertain
- have visuals that help explain difficult concepts
- create contrast and engage your audience
- be easily read and seen from the back of the room
- promote your brand, e.g. logo, contact details, social media profiles, perhaps topping and tailing your speech with slides that are shown before and after your slot.

STEP 9: PUT YOUR SPEECH TOGETHER AND TRANSFER IT ON TO A FEW INDEX CARDS

Unless you are an established professional speaker and delivering your standard keynote for the hundredth time, you will need some form of notes to keep you on track. The fewer index cards you need to use the better. The index cards are there to remind you of key phrases or transitions.

The reason for suggesting index cards, rather than a piece of paper, is that when you are nervous your hand may shake a little. If you are holding a piece of paper, this then becomes very obvious and can distract from what you are saying.

How to deliver a speech with impact

It doesn't matter how well your speech has been designed or how amazing the message you want to deliver, if you can't deliver your speech with impact, then you may as well have not turned up in the first place. Let's use an analogy. Would you pick up a scruffy, boring-looking book with a badly designed cover? If the book, then, were poorly printed with many typos and mistakes, how quickly would you stop reading and give the book up as a lost cause? It's the same with your speaking skills: your audience will stop listening to you if you can't speak with confidence and deliver your message succinctly.

EYE CONTACT

Your aim as a speaker is to make eye contact with the whole room. Similar to an actor playing to a packed house, make sure you look up towards the back of the room. Every now and then make eye contact – for three seconds each time – with different people in the audience and slowly scan the room from time to time.

> **Tip**
>
> If you are feeling nervous, look for a friendly face in the audience and make eye contact with them. They will almost always smile at you, which can help your confidence.

PAUSES

Using pauses is a powerful tool for a speaker. A well-timed pause can:

- increase the emotional impact of the story
- help you gather your thoughts
- calm your nerves
- give the audience time to digest the last point you made
- intensify the drama.

HOW YOU STAND

When you are speaking you want to seem, regardless of what is happening to your insides, outwardly confident. How you stand has a huge impact on how you appear. Remember a parent always telling you to 'stand up straight and don't slouch'? It's the same when you are speaking. Standing up straight, with your arms uncrossed, makes you appear confident and credible.

YOUR VOICE

Your voice is the main tool to get your message across in a way that compels your audience to keep listening. We are sure you can all recall a time when you had to listen to a dry presentation, delivered by a presenter with a monotone voice. How well did the presenter capture your attention and manage to keep it? Whilst we are not recommending that you try to adopt a voice or persona that is not you, aim to add some variety of pitch, volume and pace to your words. For example, if you want to emphasise a key word or phrase, you can drastically slow the pace of how you deliver these words. Speeding up how you speak can also be used to inject some enthusiasm and excitement into what you are speaking about.

The really great speakers will insert light and shade into their voice when they are speaking to:

- increase the emotional impact of their words
- gee-up the audience and get them motivated and ready to take action
- illustrate what they are talking about
- draw the audience in to their story.

> **Tip**
>
> Next time you have to deliver a speech or presentation, record yourself delivering it using a smartphone or voice recorder. When you play it back, listen for how you sound and opportunities for you to increase the audience's engagement by how you use your voice.

LOOKING THE PART

"The worst presenters were the ones in the least well-fitting clothes."

GUY CLAPPERTON, JOURNALIST

As with most things in life, when you know you look the part, very often this is all you need to sound the part to others. If you were in the audience at a speech you were delivering, what would you expect the speaker to be wearing? For example, if you were speaking at a conference, you would be expected to be 'suited and booted'. However, if you were speaking to a group of schoolchildren, you may like to soften your appearance by choosing to wear smart, but casual, clothes.

"Hosting events, as the MC, for my professional networks and associations, has allowed me to increase my visibility, profile and reputation just by being at the front of the room."

TIM LUSCOMBE, PRINCIPAL, KLO PARTNERS

TAKING QUESTIONS

When your audience ask you questions, at a very simple level, it means they are interested in what you are saying. Questions also give you an opportunity to handle any objections or explain a point in more detail. However, so many speakers dread taking questions, as these are almost always unrehearsed and unscripted. Occasionally you will get asked a question that you can't answer in a public arena, such as a very specific technical legal query. If this happens, be honest and promise to get back to the person who answered the question at a later date. When you are asked a question, ideally you should follow this process:

- clarify you have understood the question properly
- repeat the question so the audience can hear it
- answer the question
- check that the question has been answered to the audience's satisfaction.

PRACTISE, PRACTISE, PRACTISE

The main reason why most people suffer from nerves when presenting or undertaking a speaking engagement is that they do not spend enough time preparing and practising their speech. As part of your practise, do the following.

- Video yourself doing your speech and watch it back – note down what you can improve.
- Practise audibly the first three and last three minutes of your speech at least ten times – this will help to 'fix' the beginning and end of your speech in your mind, then you'll be able to start and end confidently without adrenaline and nerves making your voice wobble.

How to conquer your nerves

Many professionals find public speaking or delivering a presentation so nerve wracking that they will do almost anything to avoid it. Avoidance here is never the best policy.

Here are some tips to help you conquer your nerves when speaking.

Do more public speaking *The more speaking you do, often the less scary the prospect of public speaking. Every time you have the opportunity of delivering the same keynote, it gets easier to present.*

Do allocate time in your diary to prepare and practise your speech All too often people turn up to deliver a speech unprepared and under-rehearsed. If you know you are going to have to deliver a speech (or presentation), block out more time than you think you will need in your diary to focus on what you are going to say and how you are going to say it. That way, even if you have to cut the amount of time available for preparing for your speech, you will always have enough time.

Keep it simple The simpler your speech, both in terms of content and equipment you use, the less you need worry about it going wrong.

Take some deep breaths before you start Taking three or four long deep breaths where you slowly count to three as you breathe in, then slowly count to three as you breathe out, can help centre yourself before starting to speak.

Visualise the speech going very well Spend some time, particularly just before you have to speak, imagining the keynote going exceptionally well and the audience smiling and lapping up what you have to say.

Do some public speaking, coaching or training Sometimes our nerves are because we've never had any formal public speaking training or coaching. A good course or coach will help you feel confident as a public speaker, plus provide you with positive experiences of when you have delivered a keynote.

If you suddenly get an attack of the nerves when you are on stage Firstly, don't feel like you have to carry on regardless. For example, can you change the dynamics by taking a sip of water, looking down at your notes to reorientate yourself? Perhaps you can ask a question or do something interactive? This gives you the time to recover and calm down.

Case study 1
Tim

Tim is a consultant who had gained a reputation as an expert on outsourcing. As a result, he received frequent requests to speak at conferences. He used to hate speaking at conferences and, despite diligent preparation, he always felt that his nerves rather than him were in control of him when he was at the front of the room. Then, at one conference, everything seemed to click into place. He was in control of his nerves, the audience laughed in all the right places, loads of people asked questions and some very interesting potential clients came up to him at the end asking if he would come and speak with their company's board. Every time he now delivers a keynote, he remembers this conference and finds that he is now in control, not his nerves, of his speaking. Speaking now, for Tim, is a pleasure rather than a necessary evil.

What should be included in your speaker kit?

Your speaker kit, typically, is an extension of your personal marketing kit. It will contain everything you need to help you get booked. In addition to your personal marketing kit, it will include:

- your show reel
- details of your standard keynotes
- testimonials about you as a speaker, both written and videoed, from very happy conference organisers and audience members
- your one-pager or speaker sheet
- your introduction for conference hosts
- your standard speaking contract
- details of what you want conference organisers to provide for you, e.g. projector, microphone.

YOUR SHOW REEL

"If you don't have a good-quality video of you speaking in action, it's going to be very difficult to get booked as a speaker."

ALAN STEVENS, CO-AUTHOR OF *EXCEPTIONAL SPEAKERS* AND FORMER PRESIDENT OF THE GLOBAL SPEAKERS FEDERATION

A show reel is a short video clip that shows you delivering a speech. As Alan Stevens, former president of the Global Speakers Federation, found out, all the major speaker bureaus will look at, at most, only 30 seconds of your show reel. You need to make sure that you have video clips capturing you speaking to a large audience and them reacting in a positive way to you – i.e. rapturous applause, laughing at a joke of yours.

DETAILS OF YOUR STANDARD KEYNOTES

Your keynotes, or speaking topics, are topics that you are prepared to speak on. Ideally, these need to be aligned to your expertise and what your ideal clients want to be listening to (see Chapter 3). A keynote topic could be based on an article you have written, part of your book or a burning topic for your niche market.

Big conferences may require you to fill out a formal proposal document listing your keynote's objectives and learning points and maybe an outline of your speech. As a minimum, for any potential booker you should be able to freely provide a keynote title, handouts for the audience and a short synopsis of the keynote, including learning points for the audience.

TESTIMONIALS

Booking a speaker is, typically, a high-risk activity for a conference or event organiser. Before they approach you to book you for a conference, they will normally want to have some evidence that you can deliver for their audience. Therefore, make easily available any testimonials you have received – written or video – from conference organisers, clients and audience members.

YOUR ONE-PAGER OR SPEAKER SHEET

This is a one-page document that includes all your relevant speaker credentials. Ideally, it will include:

- your bio
- your photo
- keynote topics and brief synopsis
- publishing and article credits, including a small graphic of your most recent book cover
- speaking testimonials
- your contact information, including a website address where your show reel can be viewed.

See Chapter 4 for an example of a one-pager.

YOUR INTRODUCTION

As we mentioned earlier in the chapter, don't leave your introduction to chance. This is your opportunity to set the scene for your audience, without you personally blowing your own trumpet. Prepare your own introduction and make it available for conference organisers to download on your website. Bring a hard copy of your introduction on the day, in a large font so it is easy for any event host to read out.

INSTRUCTIONS FOR CONFERENCE ORGANISERS

When you turn up to deliver at an event, what do you need to be provided? For example, will you need a projector? A table at the back of the room to put books on? Any special dietary requirements?

YOUR STANDARD SPEAKING CONTRACT

These are the terms and conditions you would normally use for you as a speaker. Being hired as a speaker may be a very different service or revenue stream than your normal day-to-day business. As a consequence, you may like to have specific terms and conditions for you as a speaker. For example, your terms and conditions may cover, amongst other things:

- cancellation charges
- whether they are allowed to video you, and if they do, what they can then do with this video footage
- their obligations for the pieces of equipment they will provide for you.

How to successfully secure speaking engagements

"There are only two things you need to get bookings as a speaker: short video clips of you speaking and entertaining your audience, and referrals via your network."

ALAN STEVENS, FORMER PRESIDENT OF THE GLOBAL SPEAKERS FEDERATION
AND CO-AUTHOR OF *EXCEPTIONAL SPEAKERS*

Most professionals gain speaking engagements as a result of:

- referrals from their network, particularly from other speakers who have heard them speak
- conference organisers rebooking them or recommending them to other speakers
- a speaking bureau or agent securing engagements for them
- their role in an organisation – particularly if they or their organisation have a particularly strong story or topical message to tell.

Case study 2
Training Zone Live 2012

'Training Zone Live', a large UK conference for trainers, took place in London, two months before the London 2012 Olympics. As a result, the conference organisers chose an Olympics theme to book the speakers who opened and closed the conference. The HR director of the organisation, which staged the Olympics, opened the conference. Steve Backley, a prominent UK Olympian, closed the conference.

A conference organiser or booker typically will want to satisfy themselves that the speaker they book is a safe pair of hands who will deliver for their audience. As a result, they will often check you out by watching video clips of you speaking and looking at your online profile and reading your testimonials.

You can help yourself to get booked by:

- branding yourself online as a speaker, both on your website and LinkedIn profile
- having a speaker kit that you make readily available for bookers
- joining and participating in the professional speaking association in your country (for people in the UK we highly recommend the Professional Speaking Association).

SHOULD I USE A SPEAKER BUREAU TO GET SPEAKING GIGS?

A speaker bureau or speaking agent can help you get booked as a speaker. However, most bureaus will tend to focus on finding speaking opportunities for the speakers on their books, who they know they can easily sell to conference organisers. Therefore, if you don't have a high enough profile, speak regularly or already command high speaking fees, then most speaking bureaus will not be worth registering with. You may find that using a speaking agent helps when it comes to negotiating fees for you. Their job (and their share of your appearance fee) depends on them being able to negotiate the best rate for you.

SHOULD I SPEAK FOR FREE?

The speaking fraternity calls unpaid speaking opportunities 'showcases'. Only you can decide whether you will speak for free or at a lower fee than your normal charge-out rate. Until you have developed your skill as a speaker you should expect that most speaking engagements you carry out are for expenses only. However, even established speakers will offer to speak for free or at a vastly reduced rate if:

- there is a large audience of potential buyers in the room
- they want to try out some new material
- there is a good chance that this will lead to more speaking bookings or highly paid client work
- the organisation hiring the speaker can help them in material ways, such as promoting the speaker to their large mailing list
- they want to improve their speaking ability
- they are able to sell books to potential clients as a result of being at the event
- they want to help out a charitable cause by speaking at their event.

Summary

Adding in speaking to your marketing mix is a great way to attract high fees and opportunities to speak in front of rooms full of potential clients. To generate speaking bookings you will need:

- short video clips of you entertaining and engaging an audience
- a speaker kit
- a steady stream of referrals.

Action points

1 Do an internet search for people who speak on similar subjects to your niche. Find out what their typical keynotes are and, if possible, listen to them speak. What can you learn from your research? What topics are in demand for conferences? What three topics could you speak on?

2 If you struggle to present in front of people, join your local toastmasters to hone your ability to present.

3 If you feel comfortable presenting, then join your local professional speakers association to take the step up from competent presenter to professional speaker.

4 Create a one-page speaker sheet for yourself.

5   Craft your introduction for event hosts to use. Make sure you have a copy that you can give to the host on the day.

6   Create three different keynote speeches, which your target audience would pay to attend, that you could deliver as a 20-, 45- or 90-minute keynote.

7   Add a page to your website about your speaking topics.

8   Change your LinkedIn profile to include the fact that you are a speaker.

9   Next time you speak at an event, ask a friend to record you. Play the recording back and identify three things that you would like to improve next time you speak.

10   Ask event organisers that you have spoken for to provide you with a testimonial to use in your marketing materials.

11   Get a professionally produced show reel.

12   If you are finding it difficult to get paid for speaking at events, hire a speaking agent to represent your interests.

Further resources

For help with improving your speaking skills, building your speaking career and a speaking business, we recommend these resources and consultants.

BOOKS

- Davies, G. (2010) *The Presentation Coach: Bare knuckle brilliance for every presenter*, Chichester: Capstone

- Jackson, L. (2013) *PowerPoint Surgery: How to create presentation slides that make your message stick*, UK: Engaging Books

- Stevens, A. Du Toit, P. (2013) *The Exceptional Speaker: How to deliver sensational speeches*, Sandton, South Africa: Congruence Publishing

- Weiss, A. (1998) *Money Talks: How to make a million as a speaker*, New York, NY: McGraw-Hill Professional

WEBSITES

- Media Coach – speaker and presentation skills training **www.mediacoach.co.uk**
- Celia Delaney Speaking Success **www.celiadelaney.co.uk**
- Jeremy Nicholas – particularly his series of 28 training videos for speakers – **www.jeremynicholas.co.uk/dt_portfolio/speaker-training-videos**

PROFESSIONAL BODIES FOR SPEAKERS

- Professional Speaking Association **www.thepsa.co.uk**
- Global Speakers Federation **www.globalspeakers.net**
- Toastmasters **www.toastmasters.org**

9

Using PR to open doors

Topics covered in this chapter.

- The different types of PR available to you.
- What the media are looking for.
- How to organise your PR campaign.
- How to successfully pitch your article to the media.
- What a press release is and why you need it.
- How to get yourself regularly called by journalists.
- How to get yourself on TV or radio or have a regular column.
- Monitoring your media coverage.
- How to use PR to win business.
- Should you do it yourself or employ a PR professional?

Generating a profile and increasing your visibility through the media is actually easier than most people think. This chapter shows you how to increase your profile by generating PR through online and offline press, radio and TV.

> *"Put your message out, in whatever medium you can. You never know who will be listening."*
>
> ALAN STEVENS, AUTHOR OF *PING, THE POCKET MEDIA COACH* AND
> CO-AUTHOR OF *MEDIA MASTERS*

The different types of PR available to you

PR, or public relations, is defined as 'the practice of creating, promoting or maintaining goodwill and a favourable image among the public towards an institution, public body, etc.' in the *Collins English Dictionary*.

Social media has given professionals many more choices about the media channels they can use and the type of PR they can use within each channel.

The channels you have available include:

- radio
- TV
- national and local newspapers
- trade press
- online magazines, article sites and communities
- blogs
- newsletters
- video-sharing sites, such as YouTube and Vimeo
- audio-sharing sites, such as Audible and Soundcloud.

What you write, video or record for the media tends to fall into certain categories, including:

- a news item, such as a change in the law
- an information- or knowledge-sharing article, which is typically a feature item, such as '9 ways to network when you have no time to network'
- an opinion piece, e.g. 'Why the current rule changes will cause havoc'
- a letter to the editor
- commentary on an article or blog post
- a quote in an article.

What the media is looking for

Over the last ten years, the media world has undergone, and, to be honest, is probably still going through, a revolution in how people now digest its output. There is a movement towards, and many people now expect to get, high-quality news and content for free, from the device of their choosing, which is changing the face of the media. No longer can the media rely on large revenue from advertisers as so many of us choose to ignore adverts. As a consequence, many publishers are scaling back their print editions in favour of online editions supported by gated and premium content. The move from weekly, fortnightly or monthly editions to an online publication means that the publishers constantly require new content to feed the online beast. These changes to the media are definitely favourable for any aspiring Go-To Expert.

"A journalist partly approaches his written work as a form of entertainment."

GAVIN HINKS, FREELANCE JOURNALIST

Many newsrooms and publications drastically reduced their staff numbers and salaries when the recession hit and have not recruited nor increased salaries since. This means that more and more publications are relying on 'free' content from experts and commissioned pieces from freelance journalists. A trade publication that has a large budget for feature articles is now quite rare. Social media has opened up content generation channels for publishers, which are able to tap into publicity hungry professionals who are prepared to write for free.

All of these changes are resulting in many journalists chasing an ever-decreasing supply of paid-for work, with many deadlines that they need to hit.

The media's job is not to provide you with publicity. It needs to sell its content either directly for money or to attract advertisers (or both). Journalists, producers and editors are often under considerable time and financial pressure. Therefore, they are always looking for authority figures who will be interesting, easily accessible, generally available, memorable and bold with their opinions.

"The critical thing to understand when approaching a publication is that they have an audience. To feature in that publication, you must make sure that you tailor your message to suit the needs of this audience."

GAVIN HINKS, FREELANCE JOURNALIST

How to organise your PR campaign

You may want to think about a PR campaign to support a particular event, such as the launch of a new service. Before you start thinking about the publications in which you want coverage, take a step back and think about what you want to gain by the publicity, i.e. your aim for the campaign. Once you have identified your aim, then consider the tactics you will need to help you achieve your aim. Make sure, from the outset, you are measuring what you are doing.

Here are some good questions to ask yourself when thinking about your campaign.

- Who do you want to communicate to?
- What period of time do you want the campaign to run for?
- Will you have follow-up stories if you put this story out there?
- What publications will you target?

When thinking about who you will target, it is easier to start off with the smaller, more local or specialised publications before aiming for the national newspapers. Local press will tend not to touch a story if a national newspaper has already run it. However, many national newspapers will take their stories from the local and trade press.

When you have decided who you want to communicate to, and when you want to be talking to them, draw up a communications plan, which sets up:

- timescales for the campaign
- who is going to do what
- the stories and angles you will pitch to each publication and when you will pitch these.

Tip

If you want to build your profile in a particular sector, then offer to write an article for the trade press. Often they will welcome your articles, as they sometimes find it very hard to get well-written, good-quality copy. Be aware that you are unlikely to get a fee for your article and, typically, you cannot self-promote in the article.

How to successfully pitch your article to the media

"A large part of a journalist's job now is filtering out the weight of information that is out there. Therefore, you will need to somehow stand out to get their attention."

GAVIN HINKS, FREELANCE JOURNALIST

Editors and journalists are overwhelmed by PR specialists pitching ideas and press releases at them. You will need a little more than luck and an emailed press release to get your pitch noticed. Here are some tips to get your article in the media.

1 DO YOUR RESEARCH ON THE PUBLICATION, JOURNALISTS AND EDITORS

Before you pitch a story to a publication, do your homework. If it is a local media outlet, it will be interested in the local angle first and foremost. Make sure you tailor your story and your credentials to the outlet. Your pitch to the publication needs to explain why your story is relevant to the publication's readership. What problems does it solve for them? What value will it bring their readers? Why will they be interested in what you have got to say?

For example, when Suzy, an accountant and newly published author, wanted to get coverage in the local media, she started her press release with the phrase, 'Local bean counter tries her luck at writing'.

However tempting it may be, don't blanket bomb editors with your pitch by email. Identify a list of publications you want to target, not just at the current time, but ones you would like to feature in regularly. Then aim to make contact with the editor, particularly the deputy and/or features editor, before you want to place a story. Nearly all newspaper staff are on Twitter and listening out for stories of interest. They may also regularly ask for help with stories.

If the editor or journalist is not active on Twitter, then you can always email them a short note introducing yourself and attaching a short one-pager about you, a link to your blog/website, plus a list of topics that you will be able to help them out with. If you can show editors similar types of publications where you have been quoted or articles printed, then this will help you get noticed and used in the future.

2 MAKE YOUR ARTICLE VERY VALUABLE, TIMELY OR INTRINSICALLY NEWSWORTHY

"You are more likely to get published if, when speaking to a journalist or writing, you are bold, lively and opinionated."

GAVIN HINKS, FREELANCE JOURNALIST

The TV, newspapers and radio are hungry for news. That tends to be anything that involves conflict or has a human interest element. Unless the publication you are pitching your article to regularly commissions or uses features, your article needs to be timely. For example, is there a change in the law coming up? How will that affect your target audience? However, six months after the law has changed, there probably isn't going to be the appetite for articles on the 'recent' change in the law.

Try to avoid your pitch being too self-promotional. After all, the media outlet is not interested in promoting you, but providing valuable content to its readers.

3 BE BRIEF

When pitching your story to the media, you want to whet their appetite and get their buy-in before sending them everything. Save the full article and media kit until you have an editor or journalist interested in your story. Your aim is to keep the initial contact short and sweet.

Remember not to beg editors to read your email and craft an email title that invites them to open the email and read. Try to keep your email subject title to fewer than eight words and tailor your subject to the reader of the email.

4 DON'T EXPECT TO CATCH A FISH EVERY TIME YOU CAST YOUR LINE

You are unlikely to get picked up by every editor every time you pitch. Ultimately you want to have a list of publications, ranked in priority order. Then start at the top of the list and work down, until someone bites. Some publications will not take your article unless it is exclusive. If you don't get a response after a week, you may like to try a brief email follow-up. However, the reality is that editors and journalists are busy people and, if they wanted the story, they probably would have gone for it when they first saw your pitch.

It is always worth sitting down monthly and brainstorming some ideas for articles. All you need to think of is a catchy headline plus a one- to two-paragraph synopsis of the article. Circulate these ideas to the publications you want to feature in and, every now and again, you will be approached for the full article.

5 DON'T GET OVEREXPOSED

Most publications don't want to be seen to be actively promoting one expert over another. Therefore, if you have been successfully plac- ing articles or getting quoted regularly in one magazine, you may be passed over for a couple of editions. A magazine will try not to use two articles by the same person or firm in the same edition or quotes by an expert in two articles in the same edition.

What a press release is and why you need it

A press release is a factual account of a story that a journalist will use as the basis for their own article and research. The closer the press release is to the style of the publication – pitch, relevance, tone, angle – the more likely that an article will be written about it.

Use a press release:

- when you want to get into a publication
- to pitch a story to an editor (they will always ask for one).

"Say less, in shorter, crisper sentences, whilst making your point, and this is the way to a journalist's heart."

DAVID STOCH, MEERKAT PR

HOW TO WRITE A PRESS RELEASE

A good press release typically will answer these six questions.

- Who?
- What?
- Why?
- When?
- Where?
- How?

Here is an annotated example of a press release, which shows the six-question structure being used.

A high-achieving young HR consultant from Milton Keynes has been nominated for a prestigious award for his outstanding presentations to school pupils on crucial career advice. [**WHAT**]

Jakob Smith, 24, an HR consultant for HR Consulting, has been shortlisted to win the title of 'Assembly Presenter of the Year' by Countec, the social enterprise organisation that helps young people become employable through career awareness and employability skills. [**WHO**]

Jakob was nominated on the high quality and positive feedback from his presentations at various schools around

▶

Buckinghamshire on behalf of Countec. He has been particularly commended for his knowledge sharing on the key skills that employers are looking for: how to successfully apply for work experience, including top tips for interviews, and many other crucial aspects of the job-seeking process.

Jakob himself has worked across a range of sectors over his six-year career. Having left school following A levels, he worked at Tesco as a trainee retail manager, gaining exposure to a practical work environment, before moving into a generalist HR role at Premier Inn where he quickly developed his interest in HR. Jakob also gained experienced within the public and other private-sector organisations in HR roles before joining HR Consulting in 2010. [HOW]

On being nominated for the prestigious award, Jakob commented, 'I'm truly humbled and grateful to have been put forward for this prestigious award, but am very passionate about the cause it represents. To help tackle youth unemployment, I firmly believe young people have to constantly seek opportunities to learn and develop key skills so they can become valuable to potential employers. Not only will this help young people to gain confidence in their own abilities but, it will also encourage employers to put their trust in them. Young people need to be prepared to be challenged and to go outside of their comfort zone and build up as much relevant practical experience as possible. By taking responsibility for their own continued learning and development, this could help alleviate the high numbers of young people out of work. I have always taken this approach and I have enjoyed a progressive and successful start to my career. [WHY]

The awards will be presented at the prestigious award evening in early September. [WHERE and WHEN]

To help get your press release read, always send a personal note to the journalist or editor with the press release.

A good note will be short and concise and use a similar format to this.

1 A personal greeting, e.g.:

   'Dear Simon,'

2 A one-sentence pitch, which has a hook enticing them to read the whole of the note and press release. Typically, the hook will be something controversial or something unusual. This sentence will always be simple and concise, e.g.:

   'I've got this story about a local marketing expert who has written her first book, which will help new business owners reduce their first-year costs by up to 75 per cent.'

3 Then a short sentence explaining why the story you are pitching is relevant to the publication's readership, e.g.:

   'It's relevant to your readership, because the author is local to you and the small business owners who read your publication will find the book saves them, potentially, many thousands of pounds.'

4 Then offer yourself (if you are the expert quoted in the pitch) up for an interview. Plus, ask them to let you know whether or not they plan to run the story, e.g.:

   'Sam Brown is available for interview and can be contacted on 01234 567 8910. Please let me know whether or not you plan to run the story; I will hold back on offering it to your competitors for the next few days.'

5 Finally, cut and paste the press release into the bottom of the email. Don't send a press release as an attachment as it can get lost and corrupted, saying, e.g.:

   'I have included the press release below.'

Tips to get your press release read and used.

- It is OK to follow up politely. If you don't hear anything after the second follow-up, assume that the editor is not going to run your story.
- Don't send photos with your first email. Send these as a separate email, as this gives you an excuse to follow up.
- You may have more luck when pitching your story if you ring the editor before you email them the press release.
- Include an element of conflict in your story, which is prompting action from you or others.
- Use bold language in your press release.

How to get yourself regularly called by journalists

The ideal situation is where you find yourself regularly being asked to quote or submit articles or interviews to the media. It is easier than you think to get into this situation, particularly if you put yourself in the shoes of the journalist, editor, researcher or producer.

SAY YES AND BE HELPFUL

Most people in the media have a deadline to work towards. Make their life easier by saying yes and going more than the proverbial extra mile for them. What can you do to make their life just that little bit easier?

SAY THANK YOU ONCE THEY HAVE DONE AN ARTICLE

Remember that it is not the media's job to get you publicity. Therefore, show your gratitude every time they help you get publicity by saying thank you.

GET BACK TO THEM PROMPTLY

Most journalists, and particularly those involved in radio and TV, will be under the pressure of a deadline. If they can't get what they need from you promptly, they may go elsewhere. If you know that you can't help them, then say at the outset and introduce them to someone who can. Ideally, get back to them well before their deadline. Ten minutes after their deadline and your insightful quote may get left out.

DISTIL DIFFICULT CONCEPTS CONCISELY INTO A SIMPLE DUMMIES GUIDE

Although journalists tend to write for certain sectors, they are not technical experts. Therefore, they will often return time and time again to a favoured expert who they know will be able to break it down for them and explain the difficult concepts simply.

DON'T SIT ON THE FENCE

As I mentioned before, most journalists are after something newsworthy or hypeworthy, such as conflict. They are looking for people who will stand by an opinion – even if it may be different from the accepted wisdom. They don't want to work with experts who feel that they need to caveat everything they say. However, don't commit career suicide by saying something to a journalist that isn't true or could damage your credibility just for the sake of a few column inches.

Make your point, qualify it, give nuggets of insight. Pinpoint what is interesting or unusual. Make sure you are not just regurgitating what everyone else is saying.

"The middle ground tends not to be interesting to journalists."

DAVID STOCH, MEERKAT PR

IDENTIFY SOME QUOTEWORTHY PHRASES AND SENTENCES

Before the journalist interviews you, think about some quoteworthy phrases and sentences that you would like to be included in the article. Then envisage your quote sitting in the 'boxed out' part of the article. Does it work for you?

> *"I would rather that my clients give me one sentence than five sentences. Think of it as a tweet rather than a lecture."*
>
> DAVID STOCH, MEERKAT PR

BECOME A FREELANCE JOURNALIST'S BEST FRIEND

Journalists are either 'staffers' (employed by a publisher) or 'freelance' (commissioned to write articles by a publication). A freelance journalist will often tend to specialise in certain topics or sectors. Consequently, by having a good relationship with a handful of freelance journalists you could get regularly into many more publications than you can by yourself. When you talk with a freelance journalist, always find out how they found your name and whether or not they have any other articles you can help them out with. If you have been called by a staffer, do ask them if their publication has a forward features list and how far ahead they tend to be commissioning or working on features.

STAY CLOSE TO THEM

When journalists are up against a deadline, they will tend to gravitate towards the expert who pops into their head first. You want to be that expert. The best way to do this is to have a keep-in-touch strategy, which keeps you regularly communicating with the journalists and editors you want to stay close to. Twitter is an excellent tool for staying close to journalists. See Chapter 6 for more on keep-in-touch strategies.

Case study 1
Stephen

Stephen was a partner at a large consulting firm that regularly featured in the trade and national press. He achieved this feat by doing three things.

1 He always made himself accessible to journalists when they called. He would give them his direct line and mobile phone numbers, and made himself available to speak to them – almost as if they were his best client. If he couldn't speak to them, he would make a point of rearranging his call within 24 hours.

2 Stephen's area of expertise was helping large multinational firms implement large strategy changes. To help out journalists when they called, he would always send them a simple guide to implementing change in large organisations, particularly highlighting where the typical pitfalls were for companies and give high-profile examples of where this had occurred in the last few years.

3 Stephen had a knack for explaining what he did and how his expertise related to the journalist's query, very simply. Journalists found that, after they had talked to Stephen, they had a much deeper knowledge of the subject and were more confident to write their copy.

How to get yourself on TV or radio or have a regular column

This is a tough ask, even for a PR professional, simply because of getting the availability and a media outlet willing to potentially endorse you by your association. Writing your own columns or becoming a featured blogger is the holy grail of PR.

The professionals who have got the columns, who have featured blog-ger status or regularly appear on the radio or TV tend to have:

- proved they are the Go-To Expert over time
- built a very strong relationship between the editor and themselves
- been tested by the editor over time
- become an industry celebrity
- shown they are willing to contribute to the publication for free
- a boldness in their opinions.

Monitoring your media coverage

Your media coverage will help to establish your credibility for poten-tial clients and intermediaries. Therefore, you want to monitor and record all the media coverage you get.

- Keep a document listing all the media coverage you have obtained, when you got it, and by which journalist. Make sure you have a link to the piece of media coverage, so you can easily share it with others.
- Record on your website when you have 'been in the news'.
- Get a copy of any book in which you are quoted, either in the text or on the book jacket.
- Set up a Google alert on your name, your firm's name, plus topics you regularly write or talk about. We find that a Google alert often tells you when an article goes live, before the editor or journalist responsible for publishing the article does.
- Ask for PDF versions of your articles from the journalist or editor.
- Keep a physical copy of any articles or mention of you in print.

How to use PR to win business

"Now that the lines between Marketing and PR have become blurred, you can generate new business in all sorts of ways."

ALAN STEVENS, AUTHOR OF *PING, THE POCKET MEDIA COACH* AND CO-AUTHOR OF *MEDIA MASTERS*

Only very rarely will you generate an enquiry as a result of an article or TV/radio appearance. Your aim is not to generate business from your PR, but through the credibility, trust and extended reach you generate with your PR.

Here are some ideas of ways to use PR to win business.

- Send your published articles and quotes through to your network and get their opinions on the questions or topics raised in the articles.
- Include a trust panel on your website with all the key publications or programmes you have appeared in.
- Include links in your author credit and online articles to generate back-links to your website and improve your search engine ranking.
- Send key published articles through to new prospects to heighten your credibility with them before you meet.
- Send copies of your published articles through to conference/event organisers when you pitch to speak at their event.

Tip

When you have an article or quote published in a credible trade (or national) publication, send a clipping of this article with a short covering letter to the editor of another publication, introducing yourself, listing three to four of your credibility statements and stating what topics you can offer your expert opinion on.

Should you do it yourself or employ a PR professional?

Most of what we have talked about in this chapter you could do by yourself. However, everything in life is a balancing act. If you don't have the time, inclination or perceived skill to make friends with the media and pitch articles to them, then hiring someone to help generate publicity for you may be a smart move on your part. Anyone you hire must bring with them a network of the right contacts in the media, skill at pitching a story and the ability to write an engaging story.

Before you hire someone to help you with your PR, ask them:

- who their best contacts in your specialist area/sector are
- to talk you through how they secured some of their recent press coverage
- what ideas they have got for PR campaigns to help you achieve your business objectives.

Summary

Using PR to help increase your profile is easier than most professionals believe. To get yourself regularly into the press:

- actively seek out journalists, particularly on Twitter, and take the time to build strong relationships with them
- practise distilling what you have to say to journalists into short, concise, quotable phrases and sentences
- get comfortable with having a view and not sitting on the fence
- be on the lookout for newsworthy stories that you can comment on and pitch to the press
- use the publicity you generate through the media to build your credibility with potential clients and event organisers.

Action points

1   Identify a list of five to ten trade, local, online and national publications that your target audience reads. Look at the publications' websites to find the names of editors and journalists who work for these publications. Then, if they are on Twitter, follow them and start a dialogue with them.

2 Send a one-pager about yourself to editors of publications you want to be featured in, stating the topics you can credibly comment on. If you have any relevant PR include this with the one-pager.

3 Brainstorm monthly, with your peers, colleagues or coach, ideas to pitch to the media for stories.

4 Create technical briefing packs (a simple guide to your technical specialism) that you can send to journalists ahead of any interview.

Further resources

To help you generate media coverage, we recommend the following resources and consultants.

BOOKS

- Meerman Scott, D. (2013) *The New Rules of Marketing & PR: How to use social media, online video, mobile applications, blogs, news releases & viral marketing to reach buyers directly*, Hoboken, NJ: John Wiley & Sons
- Stevens, A. *101 Media Tips*, Kindle Edition

10

Successful seminar selling

Topics covered in this chapter.

- How events help you generate more leads.
- The different types of events available to you.
- The key stages in planning, marketing and running an event.

One tried and tested route to generating a reputation as Go-To Expert is to run physical or virtual events showcasing your expertise to your preferred audience. Events are a great way to help potential clients move from 'I may want to work with you' to 'Can we talk about how we can work together'. However, running and marketing events are a huge investment in time and money. This chapter shows you how you can use events intelligently to generate the maximum amount of new client work for your money and time.

"A good basic selling idea, involvement and relevancy, are as important as ever, but in the advertising din of today, unless you make yourself noticed and believed, you ain't got nothin'."

LEO BURNETT

How events help you generate more leads

Most professionals face the problem that their services are frequently high-risk, either in terms of fees or reputational risk if it goes wrong. This can prevent many clients from signing up with you because they don't have a low-risk way of trying you out. Events give your potential clients the opportunity to test out your services in a safe way. Many Go-To Experts run paid events as part of their product ladder, not to earn a profit from the event, but to help potential clients buy a big-ticket service or product.

Case study 1
Tim Luscombe

Tim is an expert in company sales and acquisitions. Virtually 100 per cent of Tim's new business comes from introducers. To facilitate these introductions, he joined networks of business consultants. To build his profile in the networks, and to be seen as an expert, he started to run workshops on different aspects of company sales and acquisitions for these networks. As a result of the profile and credibility he generated through running these workshops for the consultants, he became known as 'The Corporate Finance Speaker' and built a significant income delivering workshops and speaking on topics related to corporate finance. This has also resulted in more new business for his consulting skills.

The different types of events available to you

Technology has moved on so much that you can run events without your attendees needing to leave their offices or homes. There are three main types of events that you can run.

1 **Face-to-face seminar or networking event** This is where your attendees come to a venue of your choosing. At the event you may spend some of the time presenting or facilitating a conversation with the attendees.

2 **Webinar** This is where you try to create the interactivity of a face-to-face event via the web. Typically, attendees in a webinar have a suite of tools to help interact with the event, such as polls, asking questions, chatting via text with the presenters and other participants.

3 **Teleseminar** This is where your attendees dial into a telephone line where they can listen to you speaking. Sometimes your attendees can listen in via the web; however, interactivity is often minimal. The functionality of the software you are using to host the teleseminar may allow you to show visuals, plus allow the attendees to see you as you are speaking. However, very often teleseminars are delivered as pre-recorded sessions.

WHY USE?

FACE-TO-FACE EVENT	WEBINAR	TELESEMINAR
• You can build up trust and credibility with your audience quickly, in a way you can't do if you are not in the same room • You can network one-to-one with prospects before, during and after the event • It's easy to generate rapport, trust and credibility with your audience • You can piggyback your event on to another more established event, such as a drinks reception after a conference	• Low cost to deliver as technology cost is significantly lower than hiring a venue • Easy to get people to attend as normally there is no travelling cost involved, and less time commitment needed for people to join • You can reach an international audience • Easier to keep your audience involved and engaged than a teleseminar • Possible to reach a very large audience for your event • You can deliver the webinar at a place of your choosing – even in your pyjamas from home • Cheap to record, share and distribute to people who couldn't attend the event	• Often cheaper to run than a webinar and significantly cheaper to run than a face-to-face event • Easy to get people to attend as normally there is no travelling cost involved and less time commitment needed for people to join • Good for broadcasting a message to a very large audience • Cheap to record, share and distribute to people who couldn't attend the event • Possible to use even when your event speakers and participants can't get an internet connection • Can record the event in advance and then play it on autopilot • You can reach an international audience • Easy to turn the event into podcasts

The key stages in planning, marketing and running an event

Regardless of how and when you decide to host your event, to maximise the returns you will need to make an investment in planning and marketing, involving both you and your team.

PLANNING YOUR EVENT

There are four main steps to planning your event:

1 event goal
2 risk evaluation
3 how to achieve the event goal
4 logistics.

1 Event goal

It is foolhardy to agree to an event without first deciding on the goal for the event, i.e. what is it going to help you achieve? How will it progress your business development plans? Go back and look at the goals you set yourself in Chapter 1. How will this event help you to achieve these goals?

2 Risk evaluation

It seems a little pessimistic but, before you commit time and resources to this event, do consider what could go wrong and how you can mitigate this risk.

- What will happen if not enough people turn up?
- What happens if we can't get our first choice venue?

Your final part of the risk evaluation is to do a go/no-go analysis. What conditions will you need to satisfy to go ahead with the event? This may not be just about getting people signed up; it could also be related to the number and quality of speakers who have committed to contributing to your event.

3 How to achieve the event goal

In this step it's time to put your thinking cap on. What are the things you need to do before, during and after the event to help you achieve the goal of the event?

- How much time should you allocate to the speakers and how much time for networking?
- Who are the right people to have speaking at the event and in what order?
- How many attendees do we need to make the event a success?
- Considering our available budget, the type of service we are trying to promote, the audience we are trying to attract, what is the best format and medium for the event? Face-to-face event? Teleseminar? Webinar?
- What's the hook to help people to sign up for the event?
- Why should attendees give up the time to attend this event?
- What will we aim to get attendees to do as a result of the event?
- What will we give (if anything) attendees as a result of attending the event?

4 Logistics

The final step in planning your event is to draw up a project plan and decide on the logistics for the event.

- Where (or how) is the event being held?
- What time does the event start and finish?
- Who is responsible for each part of the event?
- How will delegates register for or buy tickets for the event? Will you use a landing page or ticket/event management software to help you?
- When will the team responsible for running the event meet to discuss progress?
- What physical things need to be produced or done for the event to be a success?

MARKETING YOUR EVENT

The hardest part of holding an event is not the running of the event, but actually getting people to commit to attend and then to physically attend the event. Combine the fact that the internet provides most people with the information that they require and people's time is fast becoming their scarcest resource, is it any wonder that it is a tough ask to get people to attend events? Even free events with highly respected speakers and delicious canapés.

Case study 2
Professional Speaking Association (PSA) 2013 Autumn MEGA Convention

When tickets for this event went on sale, one third of the total were sold within a week, 25 per cent were sold within 48 hours and 100 per cent of the tickets were sold two months before the event. The PSA achieved this feat by:

- heavily promoting this event to the delegates at their very successful spring convention
- having 50 substantially discounted tickets that the delegates at the spring convention were told about in advance of everyone else
- using a very strong Facebook community to advertise the convention daily

- tailoring the events at the convention very closely to the needs of the audience, i.e. housing established and aspiring professional speakers
- using Cialdini's principles of scarcity and social proof to influence delegates at the spring convention and in the Facebook community to buy their tickets early.[4]

Using your email list and social media community

Having a big list or large community of engaged followers makes marketing an event much easier. If people have taken the time to build up a relationship with you, and like what you talk about, they are more likely to come to an event run by you. We find that when we run an event we expect at least 75 per cent of attendees to come from emails we have sent to our lists, and under 25 per cent of attendees to come from messages we have broadcast on social media about the event.

We have found that we get a better response from emailing our list if we remind them several times about the event and create a sense of urgency by, e.g.:

- limiting the number of participants
- creating a tiered pricing structure, with the price of the event going up as you get nearer and nearer to the event
- telling people about the number of people who have signed up.

Lead magnets

These are items that you offer to your website visitors in return for them signing up to your email list. These could be a report, e-book, article or white paper, that are of *perceived value* to your target audience. Typically, this is because it solves a problem that they may have. Go back to the research you did in Chapter 3 to help you think about a good lead magnet to help encourage visitors to your website to sign up to your list.

---

[4] Cialdini, R. B. (2007) *Influence: The Psychology of Persuasion*, London: HarperBusiness.

Tips for building up your email list

- When you meet someone, ask for permission to add them to your email list.
- Offer something of value in return for people signing up to your list.
- When you are speaking at an event, talk about a report/article/guide that you are willing to give them in return for their email address.
- Run a joint event with someone else in order for them to promote your event on their list.
- Make it easy for visitors to your website to sign up to your mailing list.
- Use email marketing software, such as MailChimp, Constant Contact, InfusionSoft, Office AutoPilot, to help you manage and maintain your email list.

When can you legally sign someone up to your mailing list?

In the EU (and there are very similar rules in the USA) you can only sign people up to your mailing list if they give you prior permission or if they buy from you and you give them a chance to opt out, on every mailing.

The Electronic Communications (EC Directive) Regulations 2003 says this:

1st Rule
When they send marketing emails to you:

- the sender must not conceal their identity
- they must give you a valid address for opt-out requests.

This rule actually applies to all marketing messages sent by electronic mail, regardless of who the recipient is.

2nd Rule

Senders cannot send such messages unless they have your prior consent to do so. This strict 'opt-in' rule is relaxed if three exemption criteria are satisfied. These are that:

- your email address was collected 'in the course of a sale or negotiations for a sale'
- the sender only sends promotional messages relating to their 'similar products and services'
- when your address was collected, you were given the opportunity to opt out (free of charge except for the cost of transmission), which you didn't take, and the opportunity to opt-out must be given with every subsequent message.

This rule applies only to unsolicited marketing messages sent by electronic mail to individual subscribers.

Buying an email list

Building up a permission-based email list takes time and patience. It can take years to build up an engaged email list that numbers into the thousands. For example, it took us six months to build up 200 names on our 'How to make partner' mailing list, then another six months to increase that to 1,000 names on the list. If you don't have the luxury of time to build up your list, you may consider purchasing a list for as little as £100 for 10,000 names.

Even if you are lucky enough to buy a list of 100 per cent working email addresses, don't expect much response from your email campaign to you. Remember that these people haven't requested to hear from you. Your email in their inbox may go straight to spam and is unlikely to be enthusiastically welcomed. If you buy a list, make sure the company selling it to you guarantees that everyone on the list has actively agreed to receiving unsolicited messages by email from third parties.

Using direct mail

Before you can use direct mail you need to have a mailing list. If you have been diligently collecting your clients' and prospects' postal addresses, then you can use this as your mailing list. There is nothing stopping you finding addresses from the web and directories to create your own mailing list. Alternatively, you can rent a mailing list – expect to pay around £100 per 1,000 names. If you are creating your own list, you must check with the Mailing Preference Service that your contacts have not opted out of receiving direct mail.

The response rate for direct mail is typically about 1–2 per cent. However, if you target the mail shot well, and follow up with a phone call after the mail has landed, you can have a much higher response rate and you are more likely to get people to attend your event. If you have a large mailing, consider using a specialist mailing house to help you print and send out your mail shot. It will save you time and money in the long run.

To help increase the success of using direct mail to get people to attend your event:

- address the envelope and letter to the actual person you want to read it
- most businesses respond better to mail shots received midweek
- use a headline near to the top of the letter to highlight the key benefit to the reader for reading the email of – this headline must make the reader want to find out more
- use the body of your letter to emphasise the key benefits to the reader of attending your event
- tell the reader what they need to do next, i.e. go to your webpage to secure their place at the event
- follow up each letter with a phone call to find out whether or not the person is coming
- on the week and day of the event, send a reminder to attendees about the event.

Co-marketing and co-running events

Jointly marketing events can be a win–win for both parties. When you are new to a marketplace, co-running an event with someone who has a much larger list or more credibility with your target audience can be the best way to generate leads from events. Before you agree to co-marketing or co-running an event, check carefully:

- what you both want to get out of the event
- that the attendees will benefit from the co-operative event
- who will pay for what
- who is responsible for what – particularly getting people to sign up for the event
- what activities each of you will commit to do to make the event a success.

Case study 3
Elinor

Elinor heads up a large training and consultancy firm. The firm uses webinars to engage with current clients and prospects. It runs one webinar every two months and always starts marketing the webinar six weeks before the event. It runs the webinar with expert speakers, both from inside and outside of the firm. The firm markets the event by the following methods.

1 All members of the firm have a link to the next webinar on their email footer. Their three business development directors have a personal target to get at least five people signed up to the webinar.

2 They produce a short 'taster' and 'teaser' video with the expert speaker to generate demand for the webinar.

3 Each event has three email shots sent out to their list.

4 Three weeks before the webinar they personally ring all their clients and prospects who have not committed to attend to see if they are interested in attending.

5 Two to three days before the webinar, they ring each attendee to check they are still coming and find out what they want to get out of the event. They use this information to tailor the event.

6 After the event they ring every attendee to find out how they found the webinar and what worked for them. They use these phone calls to actively get testimonials to use on their marketing materials for future events.

▶

As a result of this process, they find that they normally get 20+ people on each webinar and, typically within 12 months, generate at least £20,000 of new business from the attendees on each webinar.

RUNNING YOUR EVENT

As your reputation and credibility are on the line with an event, you want it to run without a hitch. As a result, you need to focus on both making sure the attendees turn up and that the actual event runs smoothly.

Here is a checklist you may want to use for your event.

Technology

- Does it work on the day?
- Do all the presenters and participants know how to use it?
- Are all the slides, videos and visual materials preloaded and working with the audiovisual set-up you are using?
- Do you have a good back-up if the technology doesn't work?
- Have you told your delegates what to do if the technology stops working?

Attendees

- Have you reminded attendees a week before and on the day about the event?
- Do all your attendees know where to go and what to do to attend the event?
- Have you got an incentive for people listening in or attending a physical event to stay to the end?
- Is the entrance to the venue clearly signposted, with the name of the event on the signpost?
- What do you want the attendees to do after the event?

Presenters

- Do all the presenters know what they are doing and when they are doing it?
- Have the presenters been given the opportunity to have a dry run?
- Have you told the presenters what you will do if they start to run over time?

Event organisers

- Have all the people responsible for the smooth running of the event been briefed about their roles and responsibilities?
- Do you have people greeting attendees and briefed to keep them entertained before the event starts properly?
- Have all the name badges, handouts and goody bags been produced and where they are meant to be?

Summary

Using events can be a great way of helping potential clients take the step into commitment and sign up as a client. However, events, regardless of whether they are a face-to-face event or a virtual event, such as a webinar or teleseminar, take a large amount of time and resources to do well.

Action points

1 Volunteer to be a speaker on someone else's webinar.
2 Start building your own mailing list.
3 Revisit the pain points of your niche market from Chapter 3 and decide on an appropriate lead magnet to help build your own mailing list more quickly.
4 Research what events your competitors are hosting or participating in. Identify from your research and your niche market's pain points an event that you could host or co-host.
5 Sign up for a free 30-day trial of GoToWebinar to test out what you can actually do with a webinar.

Further resources

To help you successfully promote and run a seminar (whether virtually or face-to-face), we recommend these resources and software.

BOOKS

- Calvert, P. (2004) *Successful Seminar Selling: The ultimate small business guide to boosting sales and profits through seminars and workshops*, Oxford: How To Books
- Everitt, R. (2012) *The Complete Secrets to Seminar Success*, Jersey: Cinnamon Edge Publishing

RECOMMENDED TELESEMINAR AND WEBINAR SOFTWARE

- GoToWebinar **www.gotomeeting.co.uk/fec/webinar**
- Instant Teleseminar **www.instantteleseminar.com**

Turning leads into clients

In Part 3 of the book, we considered all the different types of marketing activity you would do to generate leads. However, once you have generated a lead, you still need to turn them into a loyal and paying client. This part of the book shows you how to convert your potential clients into loyal clients. It also looks at how to systematically manage your pipeline of potential work so that no opportunity slips through the net.

11

Managing your sales pipeline

Topics covered in this chapter.

- Building your tactical marketing plan.
- How to spot a potential lead.
- What is my sales pipeline?
- How to follow up with a lead without being pushy.
- How to get a face-to-face meeting with your prospect.
- The importance of keeping in touch with prospects and past clients.
- Proactively warming up prospects in your network.

Up until now in the book, we have been focusing on everything you need to do to create opportunities to work with these clients. This is often talked about as the marketing part of the business development lifecycle. If you follow the steps we have outlined in Parts 1, 2 and 3, you will start to gain a steady stream of potential clients ready and willing to work with you. However keen these potential clients are to work with you, you will still need to actively manage them through to a signed-up and invoiced client. In this chapter, we look at the processes and systems you need to have in place to effectively manage your sales pipeline, so that you don't lose any potential clients along the way.

In this chapter we use the following definitions.

Prospect Someone in your niche market who could be a good client for you.

Lead Someone who has proactively contacted you to talk about using your services.

Client Someone who you are currently advising for an agreed fee.

Tactical marketing plan This is something that looks at the business that you strategically need and converts it into a specific list of where you'll get it from, what activities you'll do to get it and how much business you'll get from each type of activity.

Sales pipeline *Any potential new pieces of client work that you don't yet have authorisation to start work on.*

Conversion rate *This is your ratio of leads to signed up clients.*

"I've noticed that when I am selling a lot of records, certain things become easier. I'm not talking about getting a table in a restaurant."

DAVID BYRNE

Building your tactical marketing plan

Throughout Parts 2 and 3 you have been bombarded with ideas of what you can do to actively market yourself. It's now time, if you haven't already, to commit to your tactical marketing plan – what you will do on a daily, weekly, monthly and quarterly basis to generate a ready supply of leads.

One of the first things we do with every new client is to review their whole marketing approach and help them create a tactical marketing plan. We find it is one of the fundamental steps to help a firm grow. This step is typically the cornerstone of how we help our clients increase their bottom line by at least 63 per cent.

One of our clients, a small accountancy practice, within 18 months, tripled the number of leads they received. They even spent less time and resources on their marketing than they had been doing before they started working with us. They did this by using a tactical marketing plan and having the whole practice focused on the activities within the plan.

If you have a tactical marketing plan, you will find that you avoid some of these common mistakes that professionals make with their business development.

1 Not knowing how many leads they need to fuel their practice growth.

2 Unable to identify what marketing inputs are having the most effect, for the least amount of effort. Consequently, their marketing is fuelled by random acts of marketing, underpinned by a large dollop of hope.

CHANNEL	MONTH 1		MONTH 2		MONTH 3		MONTH 4	
	BUDGET	ACTUAL	BUDGET	ACTUAL	BUDGET	ACTUAL	BUDGET	ACTUAL
EXISTING CLIENTS	3	4	3	2	3		3	
NETWORKING GROUP A	2	3	2	1	2		2	
John Doe (bank manager)	1	0	0	2	1		0	
Simon Smith	0	0	1	2	0		1	
EMAIL	1	0	1	1	1		1	
LINKEDIN	0	0	1	1	0		1	
TWITTER	2	1	1	1	2		1	
TOTAL	9	8	9	10	9		9	

Figure 11.1 Example of a tactical marketing plan

To build your tactical marketing plan you will need to know:

- your conversion rate for leads to new clients expressed as a percentage
- the average value of a new client assignment
- your revenue target.

These three figures then allow you to identify the number of leads you require, i.e:

$$Number\ of\ leads = \frac{Revenue\ target}{Average\ value\ of\ new\ client\ assignment} \times conversion\ \%$$

The next stage in building your tactical marketing plan is to decide on which channels you will use to generate the leads you require, i.e. how many will come from:

- introducers
- your networking activities
- speaking at events
- running events
- ...

When you have identified where your leads are planned to come from, you need to decide on the action you will take to generate the leads from each channel. To improve the accuracy of your tactical marketing plan you will need to:

- measure the number and quality of leads coming through each channel
- compute the conversion rate for each channel
- adjust your tactical marketing plan as you get more understanding about the return on investment (ROI) of each channel.

 *Tactical marketing plan exercise*

How to spot a potential lead

If you are going to be measuring the number of leads you get, then you need to know how to spot a lead. Remember that our definition of a lead is someone who has proactively approached you to explore if you will be able to help them. Sometimes, a lead is obvious, i.e. you get an email or a tweet from someone saying, 'I think I want to work with you' (or something along these lines). However, it isn't always that clear cut.

Typically, a prospect has to go through two or three distinct stages before they become a lead. These three stages are:

1 *awareness* they have to know you exist

2 *interest* they need to know you can help them

3 *evaluation* they want to be able to trial or test using you.

Very often, the evaluation stage will happen when you meet them or talk with them over the phone.

Here are common signs to look out for that a prospect is likely to become a lead:

- they ask detailed questions about how you work with others
- they are keen to know costs
- they will relatively easily agree to a conversation or chat with you
- they may look at your LinkedIn profile a couple of times over a period of a few months
- they will frequently engage with you on social media or with the regular marketing emails that they send to you
- they will ask interested questions about your services and the typical results you get for your clients
- they may recommend you to others and talk positively about you.

What is my sales pipeline?

The sales pipeline is a concept, which we (and many others) use with clients to represent where your prospects and clients are in the business development lifecycle. Now, an important thing to remember is that all sales go through a number of steps. Sometimes they go through fast, sometimes slowly and, occasionally, like leaky pipes, some of the leads will leak out. Your role in pipeline management is to help the person through the key stages in the process to make it easy and logical for them, so they understand what's going on. When leads know where they are at and what will happen next, that minimises the number who drop out. Or, to put it another way, that increases the conversion rate.

Typical stages in your sales pipeline will be:

- initial enquiry
- enquiry is qualified, e.g. you decide that this is a prospect you would like as a client
- initial meeting and fact-find from the potential client and yourself
- proposal submitted
- proposal accepted
- engagement letter signed
- start work with client
- first invoice paid.

Initial enquiry	Enquiry qualified	initial meeting and fact-find	Proposal submitted	Proposal accepted	Engagement letter signed	Start work with client	First invoice paid

Figure 11.2 Typical stages in a sales pipeline

	START MONTH	LIKELY VALUE	PIPELINE STAGE	MONTH 1	MONTH 2	MONTH 3	MONTH 4
JOB A	2	£20,000	Proposal submitted (50% conversion)		10,000		
JOB B	3	£50,000	Enquiry (10% conversion)			5,000	
JOB C	3	£100,000	1st meeting (20% conversion)			20,000	
JOB D	1	£30,000	1st invoice paid (100% conversion)	30,000			
JOB E	2	£10,000	Proposal agreed (90% conversion)		9,000		
JOB F	4	£100,000	Enquiry (10% conversion)				10,000
TOTAL				30,000	19,000	25,000	10,000

Figure 11.3 Weighted sales pipeline

 *Weighted sales pipeline exercise*

WHAT'S A GOOD CONVERSION RATE?

There is no right answer for 'What is a good conversion rate?' For example, if you sell a very expensive, big ticket service, you would expect a lower conversion rate than someone who sold a cheaper version of the same service. Part of the aim of your marketing is to weed out unsuitable leads before they take up your time, attention or resources.

A low conversion rate would be 5–10 per cent. It is not uncommon for a true Go-To Expert to have a very high conversion rate up above 80 per cent. However, if you are hearing that a professional has a 100 per cent conversion rate, they are probably not measuring their leads properly enough or they are not picking up all the leads they could be.

When you have established your conversion rate from lead to signed-up client, the next task is to look at the number of people who make it between each of the key stages of your business development process. You can then see where you have 'big leaks' in your sales pipeline and identify remedial action to fix those leaks to improve your overall conversion rate.

SALES PIPELINE MANAGEMENT

When you know what you have in your sales pipeline and what stage of the sales process it is, you can then do a multitude of things:

- forecast your future capacity requirements
- predict your future income and cash flow
- identify when you need to spend more time marketing to cover up periods of low demand.

Ideally you want to be producing a weighted sales forecast regularly. A weighted sales forecast will identify the value of your sales pipeline and will be weighted by the probability of the business converting, depending on the stage the prospect is at in your pipeline.

Example

Anna, a lawyer, identified these stages and conversion rates for her sales pipeline.

- Initial enquiry – 20 per cent conversion.
- First meeting and fact-find – 40 per cent conversion.
- Proposal submitted – 50 per cent conversion.
- Proposal accepted – 75 per cent conversion.
- Engagement letter signed and money laundering. procedures completed – 95 per cent conversion.
- First invoice paid – 100 per cent conversion.

Anna knew she had three live leads, each worth £15,000. They were at the following stages of her sales pipeline.

Lead A
Proposal accepted, work likely to start in March, but engagement letter not signed yet.

'weighted' value of work = £15,000 × 0.75 = £11,250

Lead B
Proposal submitted, but not yet accepted, work likely to start in April.

'weighted' value of work = £15,000 × 0.5 = £7,500

Lead C
Initial enquiry, work likely to start in April.

'weighted' value of work = £15,000 × 0.2 = £3,000

She then combined these to produce her 'weighted' sales forecast for March and April:

March
Lead A = £11,250

April
Lead B + Lead C = £10,500

Anna then used this forecast to plan her cash flow and also to check that she had enough capacity to deliver the work in March and April.

How to follow up with a lead without being pushy

Many professionals hate the thought of selling, as this implies in their mind that they need to turn into a pushy second-hand car salesperson. Consequently, they have a very hands-off approach to their leads and potentially lose many good clients by this approach.

Your aim when managing your leads through your sales pipeline is to let them set the pace, but also design into your sales process little acts of commitment from them to take them to the next stage in the process. These acts of commitment enable you to focus on the leads who are committed to proceeding and eliminate the 'tyre kickers'. Tyre kickers is a name often used to describe the professional's equivalent of the people who are 'just browsing' in a shop.

Unfortunately, tyre kickers can sometimes be mistaken for a genuine lead, because they will exhibit some of the same signs that an interested lead will, i.e.:

- be very interested in what you charge and what they get for that
- want some free advice from you (rather than actually pay for your services).

Here are ways of getting your leads to commit to the next stage in the process, whilst also weeding out tyre kickers.

- Ask them what they see as the next step.
- Check very early in the sales process that they have the budget to afford your services. An easy way to do this is to send them, before your first meeting, very broad brush costs for the typical client or service you provide.
- When asked to submit a proposal, ask the lead to commit to a quick conversation to talk through the draft outline before you spend a large amount of time writing it. This allows you to find out which leads are actually bringing the sales process to an end by asking for a proposal.
- Ask them how and when you should follow up with them if you have not heard anything.

How to get a face-to-face meeting with your prospect

Most professionals find that they need to get their prospect to commit to a face-to-face meeting or a telephone call before their prospect will become a lead. Testing the water by setting up a face-to-face meeting can help you generate more clients in two ways:

- it helps to establish a relationship and a greater understanding of the prospect, which may help you sell to them at a later date
- it may flush out a lead.

Getting a face-to-face meeting is as simple as asking for one. Yes, really. Here are ways in which you can increase the likelihood of the prospect saying yes:

- ask them after they have asked for some advice from you
- if you have been chatting for a while on social media, suggest a phone call to get to know each other better
- when a member of your network pops up out of the blue and starts chatting to you
- after they have given you some positive feedback
- suggest a meeting on a certain date as you are 'in their area'.

The importance of keeping in touch with prospects and past clients

Very often a statistic is cited that it is 7–14 times cheaper to win new work from an existing or past client than it is to convert a new prospect. In our experience that is very often the case. However, when the client engagement has finished it can be tempting to move on to the next piece of client work and forget about that client. As a result of not keeping in touch, your visibility with your ex-client drops and they may even go elsewhere for the next bit of work you could help them with.

That's not the only reason why keeping in touch helps your business development effectiveness. As we have already mentioned, the pace at which a lead moves through your sales pipeline is not controlled by you, but by your leads. Very often they may press pause because of matters completely outside of their and your control. This could be any number of reasons, such as:

- waiting for sign-off for a budget or a new budgetary year to start
- key personnel have moved or gone on holiday
- poor business performance and resultant low cash flow stopping any non-essential spend.

However, if you have done everything right up until this point, there is no reason why the lead may not press the go button again. The challenge you face is to stay in touch with this prospect/client until they are ready to press the go button.

Case study 1
Philip

Philip took over a business development department in a software company. When he reviewed the business development systems and processes, he identified that the company could significantly improve the way it kept in touch with existing customers and potential customers. He instigated a program for his team to get back in touch, via phone, social media and email, with all of the company's customers who spent over £10,000 with the company. As a result of getting back in touch, within six months his team had added over £100,000 of additional revenue from these existing large clients.

In Chapters 5 and 6 we introduced you to the importance of staying in touch with your network, leads and clients. Here are some tips to help you stay in touch:

- have a relationship plan for A-listers and key clients
- build and implement a communications plan for key accounts, e.g. how you will use your blog, LinkedIn updates and tweets to stay in touch with your network (see Chapter 5)
- ask your prospects, leads, clients and ex-clients what sort of information they would welcome receiving from you regularly
- a monthly newsletter is better than nothing, but the more valuable and tailored you can make the content for the audience, the better.

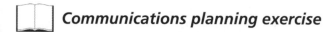 *Communications planning exercise*

Proactively warming up prospects in your network

You can use the valuable content you produce to actively warm up the prospects in your network. This content can be used in a multitude of ways, to:

- demonstrate your credibility, as well as the length and breadth of your expertise
- educate your prospect on how you have helped other people similar to them
- inform your prospect of industry trends or challenges with which they may need help.

Most professionals very rarely put in place a series of communications to help warm up their prospects. There is a health warning that goes with these communications. They have to:

- be genuinely interesting and valuable to your prospect
- have minimal sales content in them, as most people don't like to be sold to
- be tailored to the individual.

OUTLET	1	2	3	4	5	6	7	8
Newsletter				Saving tax				Succession planning focus
Blog post	Eight tips to save tax	Three ways solicitor firms make mistakes with tax	Tax planning case study	The business case for inheritance tax planning	Typical reasons for lack of succession	How to grow your own future partners	Tips to broach the subject of succession planning	Succession planning case study
Twitter	Practice management tips and topical articles for the legal profession							
LinkedIn status update	Link to weekly new blog post and topical articles for the legal profession							

Figure 11.4 Example of a communications plan

Let's emphasise that last point again. Anything that is perceived as being sent for your benefit, rather than their benefit, will be counter-productive. Within your communications plan, identify a point where you sense that the prospect would be amenable to meeting up or taking a phone call. At this point, ask them if they would like to meet.

The stick list

Your stick list is a list of the live leads you are aware of, with the next step for each lead. We recommend that all of our clients use a stick list in their business to help keep them focused on what needs to be done to progress their sales pipeline. Every day you need to review the stick list and progress any actions from it.

Summary

Every time someone agrees to buy a service from you, they go through a series of typically well-defined stages, called your sales pipeline. Your aim is to seek small acts of commitment from your lead to move them to the next stage of the sales pipeline – becoming a prospect – and ultimately have them become a client.

Your leads control the speed at which they progress through the sales pipeline – and not everyone will go on to become a client of yours. Use your keeping-in-touch processes to stay in contact with everyone, so that you maximise the chances that they become a loyal client.

Action points

1   Identify every live lead you are aware of and add these into your sales pipeline. Now calculate the likely revenue you will bill over the next 6–12 months. Will you need to increase your marketing activity or your team's capacity to hit the goals you identified in Chapter 1?

2 Set time aside each week to review your sales pipeline and identify any next steps to progress any people through the process steps.

3 Create your own stick list and review this daily.

Further resources

For more help to progress your sales pipeline we recommend the following resources.

BOOKS

- Bird, T. and Cassell, J. (2012) *Brilliant Selling: What the best salespeople know, do and say*, Harlow: Pearson Business
- Pink, D. H. (2013) *To Sell is Human: The surprising truth about persuading, convincing, and influencing others*, Edinburgh: Canongate Books
- Tovey, D. (2012) *Principled Selling: How to win more business without selling your soul*, London: Kogan Page

WEBSITES

- venture-Now – **www.venture-Now.com**

12

Honing your selling skills

Topics covered in this chapter.

- How to qualify a lead.
- How to structure and run a sales meeting.
- The difference between features and benefits.
- What to do if you are faced with difficult questions from your lead.
- Tips to help you write a winning proposal.
- How to win a competitive pitch.

The previous chapter dealt with the 'process' side of successful selling. This chapter looks at the practical selling skills you will need to convert the opportunities that come your way.

"Half the battle is selling music, not singing it. It's the image, not what you sing."

ROD STEWART

How to qualify a lead

Anything related to marketing and selling is non-chargeable time, which takes you away from doing what you love – servicing your clients. Possibly the biggest business development time waster is generating and progressing the wrong sorts of leads, i.e. the people who are never going to sign up to become a client or, if they do sign up, are not the right types of clients that you want. Now, if you have followed the advice in Chapter 3 in tailoring your services to your niche market's requirements, and our advice in Chapter 4 about positioning what you do and who you do it with, then you will filter out at least 80 per cent of the wrong type of leads. However, you do still need to make sure that, when someone enquires about using your services, they are likely to become a client and a good fit for what you do.

Case study 1
Azrights solicitors

In the last nine months, Azrights solicitors has tripled its revenue, partly due to the increased profile of the owner, Shireen Smith, but also because the firm learnt how to sell. The solicitors used to be poor at qualifying their new leads. For example, they would answer the client's initial legal question, e.g. 'How do I get a UK or EU trademark?', but not find out the reasons for the client's enquiry. This meant that enquiries, many of which never went anywhere, were deluging them. Now, if they get a new enquiry, they have put in place systems and processes to pre-qualify who they should spend the time with and who should get an email pointing them to the answer to their question. As a result of really getting to understand what their clients are trying to achieve commercially via their IP, they have found a significant increase in the number of enquiries they convert to fee-paying clients.

When you are pre-qualifying a lead, and *before* you spend large amounts of time writing a proposal, you want to be finding out about the following four things, or, DUFF:

- **D**ecisionmaker
- **U**rgency
- **F**it
- **F**unds.

DECISIONMAKER

Very often the person who enquires about using you may not be the ultimate decisionmaker. Whilst they may seem to have the right title to make the decision, it may not always be the case. For example, when we sign up clients who are sole practitioners, we often find that they need the approval of their spouse before committing to work with us. As much as possible, you need to be talking to the individual who is the budget holder and has the authority to allocate funds. When you are talking with a lead, you will need to investigate who else may need to be involved to hire you.

URGENCY

When someone buys a professional service, this normally represents a considered purchase, i.e. there is normally a high level of risk (be it money or reputation) as a result of using your services. Therefore, before you allocate a large proportion of time to developing a piece of business, you need to make sure that the lead intends to make a purchase and has a specific timeframe for doing so.

FIT

Not every client and professional adviser is a match made in heaven. Many a professional has come a cropper on an assignment due to a lack of rapport between them and the client. As well as a good level of rapport, you need to make sure the lead has specific needs that you can solve. When you first speak to them, these needs may not be easily visible. In fact, the initial 'presenting problem' is often not what, after some investigation, you end up solving. For example, we were asked initially if we could help a large consultancy firm with some confidence and body language training. As we don't specialise in confidence or body language, this at first glance looked like a poor fit for us. After just one short email exchange with the lead, this turned into strategic networking training for their fee earners. (A very good fit for us!) However, you have to determine if your potential client is truly interested to learn what is possible as a result of using your services and is motivated to achieve this.

FUNDS

As early in the sales pipeline as possible, you want to ascertain that the person has the financial capacity or access to the funds to buy from you. If they state that they don't have a budget for your services, this may not be a 'game over' sign, but indicates you will need to decide whether or not you want to educate them as to the value of your services. In an early conversation with a lead it often helps to let them know what your services are likely to cost. In this early conversation, try not to be too prescriptive with your fees, but let your lead know the likely range of fees that they may need to fork out for. For example, 'Clients with problems similar to yours typically find that it will cost them between £5,000 and £30,000 for my assistance to solve them.'

How to structure and run a sales meeting

In Chapter 11 we talked about ways to spot a lead. A key indicator that they are interested in using your services is that they will request a time to speak, either via the phone or in person. To help you get the best possible result from this meeting, we recommend that you follow this structure:

Before you meet:

- agree time, date, duration and venue
- establish a loose agenda for the meeting
- send to them your one-page credentials document (see Chapter 4)
- if you have authored a book, relevant to them, send them a copy with your compliments
- ideally, send to them a couple of pieces of valuable content that demonstrate your expertise and authority
- if you can do, start a dialogue with them on social media.

You may like to use our objective, agenda, logistics (OAL) meeting planner to help you keep your meetings focused and effective.

MEETING NAME	
MEETING OBJECTIVE	
MEETING PARTICIPANTS	
START AND FINISH TIME	

TIMINGS	AGENDA ITEMS
	Most critical agenda item
	2nd most critical agenda item
	3rd most critical agenda item

Figure 12.1 An OAL meeting planner template

OAL meeting planner

Tip

If going into a sales meeting with a corporate client, try to take someone else with you to take notes and add a different perspective to the conversation.

A week before you meet:

- check the meeting is still going ahead and reconfirm time, date and venue
- check the agenda is still the same
- ask them if there is anything that you need to prepare to help them get value from the meeting
- send them another piece of valuable content, relevant to your meeting.

When you meet:

- introduce yourself very briefly, using your sound bite
- check how much time they have for the meeting
- check that the agenda is appropriate for the meeting
- ask them what they want to achieve by the end of the meeting
- explain that you are keen to understand more about them and the organisational reasons behind this meeting taking place
- allocate at least 50 per cent of the meeting time to listening to and exploring their problems
- summarise to check understanding of what you are hearing
- identify the risks for the client of doing nothing, plus the value you can bring to the client by working with them
- find out the criteria that they will use to select a supplier
- uncover their timings and anything that will affect their ability to proceed quickly
- suggest some potential solutions
- surface any resistance or objections they may have to working with you
- agree any next steps and ask when they would like you to follow up with them if you have not heard anything.

After you meet:

- thank them for their time
- send a note summarising your understanding of what was discussed
- do your next steps from the meeting
- diarise when you should contact them next.

Tip

Don't be afraid to abandon the meeting if you realise that the lead is not a good fit for you.

The difference between features and benefits

A feature is a fact about you or your service – you can't deny it exists – whereas a benefit is something that you can *do* for the client, which the client wants. They are typically buying into the benefits of your service, rather than its features.

When you understand what the benefits are that they really want and need, then you can tailor the features to help move your lead to commit to buying from you. You can also propose solutions to help your lead achieve their desired results. However, many professionals struggle with features and benefits. In Table 12.1 see how we have turned three often used features into a benefit.

Table 12.1 Turning a feature into a benefit

FEATURE	BENEFIT
We are a national firm of accountants	We are a national firm of accountants, which means that we have the strength and depth you require to cater for all your accounting needs, thus saving you time and money and reducing the number of accountancy firms you need to engage.
We have the biggest family law department in the county	We have the biggest family law department in the county, which means that we deal with cases similar to yours every day. We know the pitfalls and can make sure that you don't fall into them. We are able to get you through the process with the minimum of heartache and angst.
We are a small firm	We are a small firm, which means that you will be a major client to us and receive a high level of personalised client service as you are very important to us.

The best way of finding out what is really important to your lead, in order to turn a feature into a benefit, is to ask them.

- What are the top three criteria on which you select your advisers?
- If we work with you, what is the main result you want to achieve?
- What initially attracted you to us, rather than our competitors?

What to do if you are faced with difficult questions from your lead

Unfortunately, good results with your clients are never guaranteed. You know that and any potential client knows that. Consequently, whenever a lead decides to work with you, they will risk their money, reputation and potential livelihood. Therefore, they are always going to want to check out exactly what is involved in hiring you and if they believe that you can deliver them what they want. When you are meeting your leads, you need to raise these concerns and, sometimes, potentially difficult questions.

Luckily, the reasons why a lead will decide not to work with you boil down to only three:

- they don't believe you are capable of doing the work
- they don't believe that they are getting good enough value if they work with you
- there is not a good relationship fit.

When you realise this, it becomes a little easier to anticipate their concerns and how these will be articulated. For example, if you were asked, 'What sorts of results have you achieved with previous clients?', this is the lead testing your ability to help them. Answer the difficult questions by using one of your credibility stories (see Chapter 4). Whilst these questions may feel difficult at the time, this is not because your lead is being awkward, but normally they either want to be reassured about something or to find out the answer to something. Changing your mindset to view difficult questions as simply a request for more information, helps you to be more relaxed in a sales meeting. It also helps you see that comments such as, 'Your fees are quite pricey' are merely a signal that they think the price is higher than that of your competition.

A good technique to use to help identify what your lead's objections are to working with you is to proactively tell them some of the objections that other clients have had before working with you. For example:

> *"Although our costs are higher, all of our clients have remarked after implementation that they now realise our solutions are robust and therefore there is no tidy-up or refinement necessary afterwards."*

When faced with one of these difficult questions, you want to let them know that not only do you understand why they feel that way but also they are right and others have in the past felt that way. In other words, you are not being defensive, but reinforcing the fact that they are right. (Remember, the lead is the one who controls the buying process and, whether or not you disagree with what they are saying, they are the ones who ultimately will decide to hire you – or not.) However, you also need to show to them that clients who had been in exactly their situation had managed to gain a positive outcome by working with you. We call this the feel, felt, found technique.

> ***Feel*** *I understand how you feel about struggling to build your client portfolio in today's tough economic climate.*

> ***Felt*** *Many of my other clients, when they were in the same situation as you, felt the same way and were wondering if they should just accept that growth was impossible.*

> ***Found*** *However, when we have worked with clients, in exactly the same place as you are now, we have found that they have been able to significantly grow their practice by taking some bold decisions and taking action.*

IDENTIFYING THE REAL BARRIERS TO USING YOUR SERVICES

Within the sales meeting, your aim is to find a mutually agreeable solution to your lead's requirements. Whilst they may raise many objections to using your services, some of these may not hinder them from signing on the dotted line. Your aim is to investigate which objections are 'real' and how to find a solution that works for both parties.

A great technique for doing this is the 'If... then...' technique. Essentially, what you are saying with this technique is, 'That's an important issue so, if we can resolve it to your satisfaction, then we can proceed to contract?' For example:

> *"If we can find a way of reducing the price by 25 per cent, then you will be happy to sign up as a client?"*

WHAT HAPPENS IF A CLIENT WANTS YOU TO REDUCE YOUR FEES

Even if you have qualified your lead correctly, there are still times when they will ask for a reduction in your fees. Unless you are in a competitive bidding situation, this isn't a showstopper, but sometimes a very good indication that you are about to sign them up.

Your aim at this stage of the process is not to arbitrarily reduce your fees, as this is educating your client that every time they want a fee reduction, they just need to ask and you will do it. You need to establish exactly the value you are delivering to them, i.e. what it is that they really want and what is a non-essential. If you can cut the non-essentials from your packaged offering, then you can offer your client a more bespoke package at a reduced fee. Your client is happy and you are happy because you have signed up a client and not reduced your hourly rate or devalued what you do for clients.

If you don't have the option to trim away parts of what you will do for the client, you may find that one of these approaches may help to eliminate the deadlock.

- Explain that the price is what it is and, if they don't want to pay that price, you will happily walk away, no hard feelings. Sometimes this works and they still sign up.
- Restate the benefits of using your services and how this will help them achieve their organisational goals.
- Demonstrate to them why it costs so much and why you don't have the room to reduce your fees.
- See if they would accept a more junior member of staff working on their account, in order to reduce their fee level.
- Use a credibility story to illustrate how other clients have also had doubts about your fees, but achieved great results, which justified your fee.
- Offer to stage payments, if they are worried about the hit to their cash flow.
- Agree a different pricing structure based on results achieved.

Case study 2
Matt

Matt is a leadership coach who had agreed a £3,000 package of coaching for a new client. The new client was getting her firm to pay the fees. Her firm queried the amounts charged by Matt and asked for a fee reduction. Matt didn't want to discount his hourly rate, so he offered a 10 per cent discount on his overall fees if the client paid up in full before he started coaching the client. His new client's firm agreed to these terms, without any more quibbling.

Tips to help you write a winning proposal

It is unusual for a lead to become a client without asking for the professional to provide a proposal. The invitation to write a proposal often brings you one step closer to a new client. A proposal, in its simplest form, is where you state what services you will provide, your fees for doing so and the objectives for working together. The form that your proposal takes could be as simple as, 'Could you just send me an email with what we have agreed to do?' or a full *War- and-Peace*-style document for a formal tender process. Here are our tips for making sure your proposals get accepted.

WHAT'S YOUR 10 PER CENT DIFFERENCE?

Unfortunately, much of what you put in your proposal will be mirrored in your competitors' proposals. The market standard is what the buyer expects from all of their proposed suppliers, i.e. it's a well-thought out, realistic, financially credible and sound proposal. Therefore, within your proposal you need to identify what truly differentiates you from your competitors. This 10 per cent needs to be the theme of your proposal – and expressed in terms of either how you will save them time and money or lower their risk in hiring you.

FIND OUT WHAT THE CLIENT NEEDS TO SIGN OFF THE SPEND

Proposals, done well, take time. Typically, the bigger the size of the project the longer the proposal needs to be. Before you start to write your proposal, ask your lead for clarification of what they, and the other decisionmakers in their organisation, will need to see to be able to sign off the spend. This means you can tailor what you write so that the key decisionmakers are able to satisfy themselves that your services are needed by their organisation. Size does matter with a proposal. Ideally, you want to keep the proposal as simple and short as possible, whilst still meeting the client's needs.

Unfortunately, it's not unusual for a lead to use the request for a potential supplier to write a proposal without any desire to buy, as a means of bringing the business development conversation to a close. It may be that the lead needs a number of different proposals to prove to their senior management that they have got the right supplier at the right price. Alternatively, it could be that many buyers know that they stop a supplier hassling them if they ask for a proposal.

If you are concerned about your lead's willingness to proceed, then ask for a small commitment before you write the full proposal. For example, this could be as simple as asking them, 'To make sure that I am on the right lines, can I jot a few points down in an email and then discuss these with you next week, before writing the whole proposal?'

If you don't get an agreement from your lead to this conversation, then think seriously about whether or not they are a serious buyer. You may find it useful to go back and qualify them again. (See the start of this chapter.)

USE A SUCCINCT EXECUTIVE SUMMARY

Very often the decisionmakers reading your proposal are time-poor. Therefore, create a short executive summary at the beginning of the proposal. In this executive summary, answer their key concerns, which are likely to be:

- cost
- time and resources involved
- expected results of doing the work.

HAVE A GO/NO-GO CHECKLIST

Writing a proposal and attending a client's premises to talk through the proposal is a big commitment of time. Very often you will find that the collective wisdom of a firm has been used to draw up a go/no-go checklist, to decide whether to allocate time and resources in response to a tender or piece of client work. A top six UK accountancy practice found that their conversion rate for new client work was 75 per cent when they had a pre-existing relationship with the client. The conversion rate dropped sharply to 25 per cent when they didn't have any pre-existing relationship with decisionmakers at the client business. As a consequence, their go/no-go checklist recommended that they go ahead with a proposal only if they had a pre-existing relationship with the client.

USE DIAGRAMS WHEREVER POSSIBLE

As the saying goes, a picture is worth a thousand words and this is very true for proposals. Many people find large swathes of text difficult to read and digest. Using a diagram may replace the need for some of the words or help people comprehend better what you are proposing.

FOCUS ON THE LEAD

Whilst it can be very tempting to outline your credentials upfront to the lead, this isn't needed and can often be off-putting to them. Typically, if you have been asked to submit a proposal, your capability to do the work is a given. When you are writing the proposal, put yourself in your lead's shoes: What do they want to hear? What do they want you to demonstrate? How are you going to address their issues?

USE A PROPOSAL DOCUMENT TEMPLATE

As mentioned in Chapter 5, having standard templates within your firm can help you increase your efficiency and effectiveness. Wherever possible, use the firm's proposal document template to help you structure your proposal and cut down the time taken to write it. However, do make sure that you tailor any standard pieces of text in the template to fit the piece of work you are bidding on to win.

QUANTIFY THE RESULTS THE LEAD CAN EXPECT FROM ENGAGING YOU

Your lead is buying results. Therefore, quantify as much as possible the likely results you expect they will get if they work with you.

PROOFREAD THE DOCUMENT MULTIPLE TIMES

Particularly in a competitive pitch situation, it's the really small things that can make or break your case for being hired. Therefore, make sure that your proposal document is completely free of typos and errors.

GET FEEDBACK ON YOUR PROPOSAL

In your project planning, allow a day for you to reflect on your proposal before sending it off to the client. If possible, ask for feedback from a trusted set of peers or colleagues on your proposal.

KEEP THE OPTIONS TO A MINIMUM

It can be very tempting to present your lead with myriad options and solutions in your proposal. This can have a similar effect to going into a shop and being so overwhelmed by the choice that you get caught up in the decisionmaking, consequently walking out of the shop having not bought what you originally intended to buy. If the lead has requested you detail different options in your proposal, keep the options to a maximum of three.

MAKE SURE THAT THE PROPOSAL IS READABLE

The proposal that you write should be simple and easy to read. Remember that your lead may not be an expert in what you do, so eliminate jargon from the document. As you write the document, imagine you were sitting opposite the person and having a conversation. Aim to keep the tone of the document conversational, rather than dry, stilted and stuffed with corporatese.

The headings of your proposal should flow together and tell a story. You may find it useful to use a technique called storyboarding, which is used in the film industry. Storyboarding is where you build up the point you want to make using a sequence of pictures or headings. When you have the pictures or headings in the right order, you then develop each heading further.

FEATURES AND BENEFITS

Wherever possible, go through your proposal document and turn any feature into a benefit for the lead. The three benefits that your buyer will be interested in are:

- saving them time
- saving them money
- reducing their risk in hiring you.

For example, instead of stating, 'We are the Go-To Expert for...', turn this into, 'You know you will be in safe hands and reduce your risk on this project with us, as we are seen to be the Go-To Expert for...'

If you know that your lead is considering working with other advisers, then you need to make sure your proposal articulates why the lead should choose you rather than your competitors. However, you need to do this in a way that doesn't rubbish your competitors. When you are speaking with your lead, find out their top buying criteria for selecting a supplier. Then show in your proposal how you meet these buying criteria.

How to win a competitive pitch

Very often large pieces of work will involve a potential client inviting many firms to submit a tender for a piece of work. The pool of suppliers asked to tender could be as few as two or as many as hundreds. Normally the lead will shortlist firms and invite them to pitch or, as they call them in the business, 'a beauty parade'. In an ideal world you would not be in a competitive pitch situation. If you follow our advice in Parts 2 and 3 of this book, you may find that your Go-To Expert status reduces the number of competitive pitches you are involved in.

It's probably best to think of your pitch as an audition. The lead literally is trying you on for size and seeing how you interact with them. Here are our tips to help you win your pitch.

BRING ALONG THE WHOLE ACCOUNT TEAM

Your client is probably wise enough to know that the partner or senior fee earner in the department is unlikely to be doing the donkey work on their account. Therefore, as much as possible, assemble a pitch team of people who actually will be working on the account.

PRACTISE YOUR PITCH AS A TEAM

It's not unusual for pitch teams to only get together on the morning of the pitch and rehearse what they are going to say in a taxi on the way to the client. One of our clients, a top 100 law firm that had a core of large UK public-sector bodies, had found that their ability to win at a pitch had dropped from 1 in 3, to 1 in 8. They found that a key reason for them losing out – particularly as their pitch teams often came from different teams and offices – was that they didn't come across as a team in the pitch. As a result, the client allocated time for a pitch team to practise and rehearse together, both via conference calls and in person. As a result of this change, their win rate increased back to 1 in 3.

Tip

When practising your part of the presentation, audibly practise the first and the last three minutes of the presentation at least ten times. This will help you to eliminate any wonky voices or nerves at the key points of your presentation. You will also come across as engaging and polished.

SHOW PASSION

Your lead wants to know that you will care about their business. Consequently, you need to show passion and enthusiasm for working on their account.

IT'S NOT ABOUT YOU

In the pitch your aim is to build up rapport with the lead and show that you really understand them. Therefore, focus your message on how you plan to solve their business problems and the results they can expect if they work with you. Your pitch is not the time to re-emphasise your credentials – let your pitch and tender documentation do that. If you focus too much in your pitch on how great you are, this can act as a turn-off for the other person.

INVOLVE THE AUDIENCE IN THE PRESENTATION

In a competitive pitch situation the lead is as concerned about the rapport and chemistry between you as well as the solution you are proposing. Therefore, treat the pitch as a conversation rather than a very formal stand-up presentation. Aim to spend one third to half of your allowed time on questions.

MANAGE YOUR TIME

Particularly in a beauty parade scenario, you will be given a set amount of time for your pitch. Many clients will not give you extra time if you run over, particularly if you are pitching to a public-sector procurement team. Therefore, use your dry run throughs to time yourself and make sure that you leave enough time for detailed questions at the end of your presentation.

Summary

Before you decide to pursue a lead, you need to make sure that you have the agreement of the decisionmaker at their company and the potential client has:

- got the budget to work with you
- the right fit for you
- enough internal urgency to pay for your services.

Potential clients are looking to work with advisers who are able to solve their problems, at the right price and time. Your role in the sales meeting is to get a detailed understanding of the lead's problems and propose a solution that the lead is motivated to buy.

Action points

1. For the next three leads who contact you, decide to pursue them based on the four qualifying criteria, i.e. DUFF: decisionmaker, urgency, funds, fit.

2. Next time you are asked to submit a proposal, suggest that you jot some ideas down in an email about what to put in the proposal and get commitment from the buyer to discuss these ideas.

3. Get out the last five proposals you wrote. Based on what you have learnt in this chapter, and which ones were successful, decide what you will start, stop or continue doing to get more proposals agreed by a lead.

4. When faced with an objection at a sales meeting, use the feel, felt, found technique to successfully handle the objection.

5. Accompany someone who is more experienced in business development than you. Watch and listen to them in the sales meeting. What can you learn from what they do in the meeting to improve your own ability in sales meetings?

6. If you have a lead asking for a reduction in fees, see how you can repackage what you are offering to them so that they get the reduction, but your hourly rate is still honoured.

7. Next time you are involved in a pitch, allocate at least half a day to practising your pitch with your pitch team.

Further resources

We recommend these books and websites to help you improve your sales skills.

BOOKS

- Bird, T. and Cassell, J. (2012) *Brilliant Selling: What the best salespeople know, do and say*, Harlow: Pearson Business
- Green, C. H. (2006) *Trust-Based Selling: Using customer focus and collaboration to build long-term relationships*, New York, NY: McGraw-Hill Professional
- Maister, D. H., Green, C. and Galford, R. (2002) *The Trusted Advisor*, New York, NY: Free Press
- Pink, D. H. (2013) *To Sell is Human: The surprising truth about persuading, convincing, and influencing others*, Edinburgh: Canongate Books
- Searcy, T. (2009) *RFPs Suck!: How to master the RFP system once and for all to win big business*, New York, NY: Channel V Books
- Tovey, D. (2012) *Principled Selling: How to win more business without selling your soul*, London: Kogan Page

WEBSITES

- The Trusted Advisor Blog **www.trustedadvisor.com/trustmatters**
- Principled Selling **www.principledselling.org**
- venture-Now **www.venture-Now.com**

The business of your brand

In the final part of the book, we look at how to grow a business around your brand. As your reputation and client portfolio grow, there will be points where you will need to think or do things differently to get to the next level. In this part of the book, we identify where those points will be and what you will need to do to get over these hurdles to maintain the growth of your client portfolio.

13

Curing the growing pains

Topics covered in this chapter.

- Managing growth.
- The five phases of client portfolio growth.

Your brand is a business – whether or not you are self-employed. If you are going to get the maximum return for your investment in your brand, you will need to think about it as if it is a business. It doesn't matter whether you are an accountant, lawyer, consultant, key account manager or other professional, anyone who sells their time for money will go through distinct phases in the growth of their client portfolio. This chapter identifies each phase and gives you ideas and remedies to help you reach the next phase of growth.

> *"Don't be a bottleneck. If a matter is not a decision for the President or you, delegate it. Force responsibility down and out. Find problem areas, add structure and delegate. The pressure is to do the reverse. Resist it."*
>
> DONALD RUMSFELD

Managing growth

Anyone who manages a client portfolio will see their portfolio grow through five distinct phases. Normally, in order to move from one phase to the next, you will have to change how you work and the resources around you. Consequently, it can be pretty difficult at times to move between the phases and, sometimes, to get to the next phase it can feel like you are taking a step back. For example, growth normally stalls for a short period of time when you hire your first team member to help you service your clients. There are five common phases you will see a professional transition through.

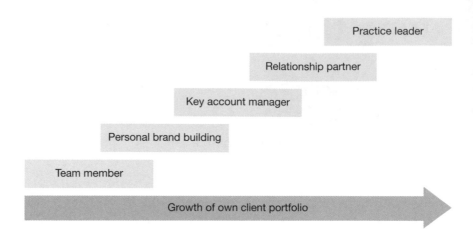

Figure 13.1 The five phases of client portfolio growth

The five phases of client portfolio growth

PHASE 1: TEAM MEMBER

Phase 1 is where you find yourself being a team member for someone else and helping them build their own client portfolio. This could be as a freelance member of a team, an interim or a junior fee earner in a professional practice. Many professionals who struggle to sell and market themselves get stuck in this phase. Whilst there is nothing wrong with staying in this phase, many professionals find the rewards and freedom of having their own client portfolio more financially and personally satisfying. Sometimes a professional – e.g., an associate with a high chargeable time target in a consultancy firm – finds that all their available time is taken up with servicing other fee earner's clients.

To move to the next phase, you need to commit to differentiating yourself from your peers and choose to sell and market yourself. This will involve taking three actions:

1 allocate the time to building your own client portfolio
2 decide on what is going to be 'your thing' (see Chapter 2)
3 create a roadmap for yourself to build your own client following (see Chapters 1 and 16).

Case study 1
Chloe

Chloe was a newly promoted associate in a medium-sized law firm. Up until this point in her career she had focused on building a broad skill base in her chosen field of employment law. She noticed that her department was getting in increasing numbers of clients who had been compromised out of their previous job. She asked her partners if she could receive these cases, as she was passionate about making sure that these clients were treated fairly and honourably by their previous employers. Over a period of 12 months Chloe came to be seen as the department's expert on compromise agreements and was asked to run seminars for local employers on the subject. As a result, she found that she started to attract her own clients directly.

PHASE 2: PERSONAL BRAND BUILDING

Once you have taken the plunge and decided to build your own client portfolio, you will need to be able to market and sell yourself, i.e. build up a desire from others to work with you. To be successful at winning your first few clients you will need to differentiate yourself from your peers and market services in a way that clients want to buy. Many professionals find that they never feel comfortable at marketing and selling themselves, so will often stay in Phase 1 or only maintain a small client portfolio of their own. This is probably the hardest phase to move out of.

To move to the next phase, you will need to:

- truly commit to your niche (see Chapter 2)
- identify a mix of services that appeal to your clients (see Chapter 3)

- build your profile and reputation, both online and offline (Parts 2 and 3)
- learn to manage your sales pipeline and convert prospects into clients (Part 4).

Case study 2
Giles

Giles was a freelance trainer who got 95 per cent of his work from training companies using him as an associate for their clients. Whilst he enjoyed the work he was given, he wanted to build up some clients of his own. Before he turned freelance he had spent most of his career in financial and professional services, specialising in leadership and team development. He noticed that, when he spoke to his ex-colleagues, a hot topic for them was how to develop virtual teams. As a result, he decided to become the expert in virtual team development for financial and professional services companies. He tailored his existing website, blog and services to help financial and professional service firms develop high-performing virtual teams. He made sure that his Twitter bio and LinkedIn profile clearly stated his niche. As a result of regularly sharing valuable content around developing virtual teams, he started to attract enquiries about using his services. Eighteen months after committing to his niche, Giles found that he had increased his income by a third, worked fewer days and enjoyed a 50:50 split between associate work and his own clients.

PHASE 3: KEY ACCOUNT MANAGER

When you have cracked marketing and selling yourself and built a personal brand that attracts your own clients, you will find that you have run out of time. There are not enough hours in the day to service your existing clients and go out and win more to hit the targets you set yourself. You will now need to move into a key account manager role and build a team around you to deal with the back-office tasks, i.e. all the non-client-related jobs that need to be done to keep the business ticking over – recording your expenses, managing your diary, etc. If you work in an established professional practice, you will probably find that the back-office team is already present.

To find more time to grow your client portfolio and move to the next phase, you will need to:

- identify anything you do that is not billable to the client and could be delegated to others; process and systemise these tasks before delegating them to someone else
- recruit, train and build up your back-office team, e.g. your virtual or personal assistant or marketing coordinator (see Chapter 14).

Case study 3
Blayne

Blayne runs his own surveying business. He always had outsourced his bookkeeping and accounting needs to a local bookkeeper and accountant. For many years his business had ticked along, until he started a relationship with an up-and-coming local builder. As a result of the work that he got from this builder and not wanting to turn any work down, Blayne found he had too much work and was doing long days to keep on top of his workload. His coach suggested that he hired a personal assistant who could run his diary for him and help him keep his blog and website updated. As a result of bringing in a personal assistant, he was able to reduce his personal workload, lower his stress levels and actually take on more work.

PHASE 4: RELATIONSHIP PARTNER

In many ways this phase is similar to the previous phase; you have once again run out of time to carry on growing your client portfolio. The only way you will create more time is to move from a key account manager role to a relationship partner role for your client portfolio and delegate or outsource client-facing tasks to a team of fee earners. This is a lot harder than delegating tasks to a back-office team, as many clients have such a strong emotional connection with you, they refuse to work with anyone else.

To break this emotional connection and move into a relationship partner role, you will need to:

- introduce team members to the client early in the business development process
- recruit and develop fee earners within your team, whether on a permanent or freelance basis (see Chapter 14)
- include the other team members in communications to prospective, new and existing clients, e.g. your newsletter, blog, tweets
- be honest with your clients about when you will be working on their business and how the role responsibilities will split between you and your team
- agree with your clients how the communication channels will work between their team and the members of their account team
- increase your own charge-out rate to make it more attractive for clients to have junior members of the team working on their account.

Case study 4
Mary

Mary had a strong back-office team supporting her as the sole fee earner in her practice. As a result of writing a book on her specialist area of outsourcing, she found that her business grew rapidly over a period of six months. Whilst Mary was thrilled that the book had been so successful, she was struggling to keep up with all the new projects she was winning. As a result of this growth, she hired a junior member of staff and started to use a highly skilled freelancer to help her with the more complex work. Initially, Mary found it hard to delegate to her team and had to hold back on the desire to tell her new team to do it 'her way'. It took a while for Mary to become completely comfortable explaining to her new clients that her team typically would do the work and she would oversee them. As a result of expanding her team and increasing her own charge-out rate, Mary was able to double the business's turnover in two years without impacting her profit margins.

PHASE 5: PRACTICE LEADER

Inevitably, as your client portfolio grows, you will once again run out of time to be able to personally run all the accounts of your clients. If you are going to carry on growing your client portfolio, you need to develop or bring in other fee earners who can go out and win their own clients.

To succeed as a practice leader, you will need to:

- develop other people in your team to take over your responsibilities as an account manager (see Chapter 14)
- take on a leadership and strategic role within your practice.

Richard was an audit partner, specialising in property companies in a mid-tier accountancy practice. Over a period of five years he steadily built up his own £1 million+ client portfolio. He noticed that his secretary was really struggling to find time for him to regularly speak to all his clients. Whilst he loved going out and winning new clients, he realised that he had hit a limit on the size of his client portfolio. He reviewed his client portfolio and formally handed over his 20 smallest accounts to a newly promoted ambitious senior manager on his team. By freeing up this space in his diary, he was able to use this time to help his senior members of the team win their own clients.

Summary

There are five distinct phases a professional goes through as they grow their client portfolio. When you know what phase you are in, you can then change how you work in order to get to the next phase.

Action points

1 Identify which growth phase your portfolio is in and what three things you can do to accelerate the development of your client following so you can move into the next phase.

2 Talk to your mentor to find out how they got through the current phase you are in.

Further resources

To help you grow your client portfolio through the five phases, we recommend that you read the books listed below. There is also a list of websites, which we recommend you visit to help you grow your client portfolio through the five phases.

BOOKS

- Delong, T. J., Gabarro, J. J. and Lees, R. (2007) *When Professionals Have to Lead: A new model for high performance*, Boston, MA: Harvard Business School Press
- Maister, D. H. (2003) *Managing the Professional Services Firm*, New York, NY: Free Press
- Maister, D. H., Green, C. and Galford, R. (2002) *The Trusted Advisor*, New York, NY: Free Press

WEBSITES

- *How to make partner* **www.howtomakepartner.com**
- *venture-Now* **www.venture-Now.com**
- *Partnership Potential* **www.partnershippotential.co.uk**

14

How to build your team

Topics covered in this chapter.

- How to build and develop a team.
- What motivates people.
- How to give effective feedback.
- What is SBO?
- How to receive feedback.
- Setting goals and objectives.
- Why you need a support community.
- Who you need in your support community.

As we discovered in the last chapter, regardless of whether you are an owner of a professional practice or an up-and-coming star, you will need a team around you to support you and to delight your clients time and time again. In fact, your very reputation as the Go-To Expert hinges on how well your team can deliver for you and your clients. As well as the people who help you deliver the client work, you will also need a support community, composed of people who are drawn from your personal, professional and family network. All the members of your support community have an important role to play in helping you achieve your career, business and life goals. Throughout your career, you will need influential people in your network who will be acting as an advocate for you. In this chapter, we provide the information that you need to build the right team and support community around you, so that you can be at the top of your game every day.

> *"Business success has little to do with remarkable service and everything to do with how you manage your people."*
>
> JULIAN SUMMERHAYES

How to build and develop a team

> *"All of us perform better and more willingly when we know why we're doing what we have been told or asked to do."*
>
> ZIG ZIGLAR

If you are going to enjoy the fruits of your labour you will need a trusted team of people to whom you can delegate work. This could be people inside your firm, outsourced support or other professionals you partner with on the assignment. This means that you will need to build and develop teams and individuals who will be able to service the work you and others bring into the firm. The teams you lead will vary in size, longevity, location, composition, performance and effectiveness.

The quality of the team you build is just as important as the quality of your client portfolio. A motivated and capable team around you will free up your time to focus your energies on building your profile and visibility, winning work, leading your part of the firm and progressing your career. Typically, a team – as opposed to a group of people – will share a mutual purpose, e.g. service all the firm's residential surveying clients, similar performance goals and hold themselves mutually accountable.

You will often hear the phrase 'high-performing team' bandied about. A high-performing team is one where:

- the whole team is focused on achieving the team goals
- the team has shared values, standards and beliefs
- there are clearly defined roles and responsibilities for each of the team members
- the team achieves superior results
- there is a high level of respect and mutual trust within the team for the skills, knowledge and expertise that each team member brings along
- the team is excellent at overcoming any obstacles so as to achieve the team's goals
- open and clear communication is present between the team members, regardless of their location in the world
- effective decisions are taken at the right time by the right people
- there is a collaborative and positive atmosphere between the team members
- conflicts are surfaced and resolved quickly and effectively.

Your role as the Go-To Expert is to build and lead your own high-performing team – after all, you will not be able to service all the client work and administration by yourself. Typically, as a team leader, at any one time, you will be performing three roles within the team.

1 *Direction finder* You will be working with your team to identify, clarify and build commitment to achieving the team's ultimate goal, e.g. bill £1 million in the next 12 months. Part of your role is to help the team identify the right journey for you as a team to achieve the ultimate goal.

2 *Facilitator* You will be helping your team members to work together effectively and knit together as a high-performing team.

3 *Coach* Similar to any sports team coach, you will be working with the team as a whole and on an individual level to make sure that people have the right skills and behaviours for the job they are required to do.

Case study 1 GreenStones

Simon Chaplin, who heads up GreenStones, an independent accountancy firm in Peterborough, attributes part of his success in the last two years to restructuring how he managed and ran his team. He was able to free up a considerable amount of his management time by clearly making the link for the team between their performance and their reward. He instigated a results-only work environment, where his team's pay (and jobs) depended on the targets they identified and hit, rather than the amount of time they billed on the clock. In order to set up this new way of working, Simon sat down with each member and helped him or her see how they contributed in their role to the success of the practice. His team are not tied to a set number of working hours, but measured and rewarded on their ability to get the outcomes the firm needed. As a result, the team members are more engaged, motivated and productive because they are in control of their work life.

Your team does not become a high-performing one overnight; it takes time, focus and energy to get it to this level. The Tuckman model of team development explains that, as the team develops maturity and ability, and relationships establish, the leader must change and adopt different styles of leadership. In the model, there are five distinct stages of team development:

1 forming
2 storming
3 norming
4 performing
5 adjourning.

FORMING

At this stage, the team is very new and freshly formed. Every time someone joins or leaves a team, the team reverts to this stage again. The team members look to the team leader for guidance and direction, plus clarification on each team member's role and responsibilities. As a team leader, be prepared to be very 'present' with the team to communicate their purpose, objectives and facilitate any external relationships.

STORMING

The team is becoming clear on its purpose and how to get there. However, there is still plenty of uncertainty and decisionmaking may be slow within the group. Inevitably, there will be some conflict as people within the team jockey for positions. Sometimes you may find that there may be power struggles and challenges to the team leader's authority. A team may never get through the storming phase where unresolved conflict is left to fester. It is the team leader's role to focus the team on its goals and resolve relationship and emotional issues.

NORMING

Only if conflict is resolved from the storming stage does the team move on to norming. The team now is fully committed to its mutual purpose and goals. The dust has settled, meaning that roles and responsibilities within the team are now clear and accepted. Collaboration across the team is established. Unlike the storming stage, big decisions are taken as a whole team, whereas the smaller decisions are delegated to the appropriate people within the team. You may find that the team is starting to socialise outside of the working environment. At this stage the team is working together to develop its working processes and team dynamic.

PERFORMING

When the team starts to display the characteristics of a high-performing team it moves to performing. The team leader role is still generally required as the team will still need ongoing coaching, delegation and guidance from the team leader. However, generally, the team is self-supporting, i.e. the team no longer needs much instruction or assistance as it is pretty much self-sufficient.

ADJOURNING

This is where the team breaks up, as it has fulfilled its purpose. If the team has been particularly strongly bonded, the ex-team members may experience a sense of loss during this stage. As a team leader it is your role to celebrate the success of the team and facilitate team members' journeys on to new projects and roles.

What motivates people

To get your team members to perform to the best of their abilities you will need to know how to motivate them, i.e. find out what makes them 'tick'. Different things motivate different people and these may change as they grow older and their lives change.

Typically, you will find that three simple things motivate most professionals:

- career progression
- interesting and challenging work
- feeling valued for who they are.

To help your team progress their career, you can:

- provide on- and off-the-job training
- coach them on the job, helping them gain new skills
- set meaningful targets for their career progression
- provide timely and regular feedback on their performance.

Being able to provide interesting and challenging work is not always easy within a professional services firm. Many lawyers can tell stories about the number of days that they had to spend photocopying as a trainee. However, when you get to be the Go-To Expert you have greater control over who gets what work. So, give some thought to the following kinds of questions.

- For each team that you lead, do you know what kind of work each team member likes and wants to do more of?
- Are you aware of the skills gaps in your team and do you have a plan in place for your whole team to be able to fill these gaps?
- What can you delegate from your desk to your team?
- Have you identified and agreed stretching objectives for all your team members?

Making people feel valued is an interesting one because not everyone feels valued in the same way. Further, you may not yet be in a position in your firm to influence some of the tangible rewards, such as a pay rise, in recognition of the value your people bring to the firm. Here are some simple ways in which you can help people in your teams feel valued:

- take an interest in what they do both inside and outside of work
- give regular praise (when it is due)
- show individuals why their work and efforts matter
- spend time with them during the working day to help them achieve their goals and objectives
- create an atmosphere of mutual cooperation
- truly listen to your team members' ideas and concerns – don't just brush them off as being unimportant.

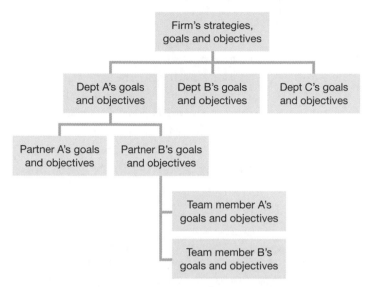

Figure 14.1 How your team members' goals and objectives relate to the firm's strategy and headline performance goals

How to give effective feedback

Giving actionable feedback is one of the most powerful ways to develop your team and yourself. So, what do we mean by *effective* feedback?

Effective feedback is feedback that:

- creates and delivers a specific message based on observed performance
- describes specific behaviour so that a person can learn by repeating good behaviour or ceasing bad behaviour
- enables the receiver to walk away understanding exactly what he or she did and what impact it had on you or others.

There are many models or processes around of how to give feedback to someone. We recommend you hold a private discussion using the situation behaviour outcome (SBO) feedback model.

What is SBO?

The SBO model is a feedback model that can be used to structure both positive and constructive feedback. Its structure increases the likelihood that the feedback will be received in a clear, non-defensive manner by the recipient. Feedback models often require you to deliver both positive and negative comments. In our experience these models never tend to work very well because the person receiving the feedback always wonders if the positive feedback is genuine and only really hears the negative feedback.

THE SBO MODEL

Describe where and when the observed behaviour occurred and what happened. Remember to be specific.

Behaviour Describe what you saw or heard. Avoid interpretations and judgements, such as, 'You weren't listening to me.' Simply describe the person's behaviour: 'When I was talking, you pushed your chair away from the table and gazed out of the window.'

Outcome Share with the individual the outcome or impact of the behaviour on you and/or on others. The outcome is what you or others experienced. It can include work outcomes, client satisfaction, work team and/or the larger firm. Most often, it starts with 'I felt...' or 'I was...' or 'It appeared to me that others were...'

Some examples of using SBO feedback:

Weak feedback 'Janet, you were good in the client meeting today – thanks.'

Effective feedback 'Janet, at the client meeting this afternoon **[SITUATION]** you demonstrated your knowledge of our aerospace client particularly well when you talked about trends in their sector this year **[BEHAVIOUR]**. The client commented on your thorough preparation and that it portrayed true professionalism **[OUTCOME]**.'

Weak feedback 'James, the office manager is unhappy – you just didn't deliver or meet his expectations.'

Effective feedback 'James, the office manager, George, on the job appraisal forms, has suggested that you weren't proactive in meeting his expectations **[SITUATION]**. Specifically, when I talked to him, he said that, despite your work being thorough, you provided reports late on two occasions without letting him know **[BEHAVIOUR]**. This led to a lot of frustration on his part **[OUTCOME ON MANAGER]** and detracted from what has been a successful job **[OUTCOME ON INDIVIDUAL]**. Can we work through this together so that we can prevent this happening again?'

Some tips for giving feedback that will be accepted first time around:

- ask the other person first what they thought went well and not so well
- praise in public, criticise in private
- always ask permission to give the feedback; unsolicited feedback is rarely welcomed
- wait until your emotions have calmed down before giving feedback
- use the SBO model to help you be specific.

How to receive feedback

Feedback, particularly when it is of the tough variety, can often be hard to swallow. The best way to view feedback is that it is a gift, but one that you can choose to act on, or not.

If you are fortunate enough to receive feedback, regardless of whether it is negative or positive:

- always thank the person afterwards (whether or not you agree with it); people offering feedback are almost always well-intentioned
- listen carefully to what they are saying, if necessary asking for clarification
- resist the temptation to get defensive or clarify your version of events

- if you feel yourself getting emotional, request some time to reflect on the feedback before discussing it.

Setting goals and objectives

Your role as leader of a team is to work jointly with each of your team members to set goals and objectives. These objectives, when combined across the team, will enable the whole team to hit its goals and you to gain the rewards from being the Go-To Expert. Your team's goals will need to cascade from your department's goals, which will flow from the firm's business goals for the year. See Chapter 1 for more detail on setting meaningful and motivating goals, milestones and objectives.

Why you need a support community

The commitment to be the Go-To Expert is a very serious intent – and at times will be all-consuming. As you will have already seen in this book, this isn't something you can achieve in isolation by yourself. This is why you need a support community. They will be at your side throughout your journey to becoming the Go-To Expert. For example, they:

- allow you to see the wood for the trees
- buck you up when your commitment and motivation to achieve your business, career and life goals takes a dip
- help you celebrate your successes
- commiserate with you when you hit bumps in the road
- provide contingency plans for your life in and out of work.

Who you need in your support community

Everyone's support community will be different and will depend on whether you are self-employed or employed within a firm. However, we suggest that an effective support community will have people playing five different types of roles.

Mentor Having someone in your support community who is more experienced can act as a sounding board and provide objective guidance and feedback is essential.

Coach Your own coach helps you to take time out from the hurly-burly of your work life to focus on what really matters to you. They will also work with you in acquiring the key skills and knowledge required to become the Go-To Expert.

Family Having a supportive and happy home life is important, if you are to become a well-rounded individual who is properly equipped to handle the stresses and strains that are part and parcel of the everyday life of a professional adviser.

Friends inside of work You are going to be at work for a significant part of your working life. If you are going to enjoy your work, then you need to have friends who you work with, whether or not you are self-employed or work for a firm.

Friends outside of work Good friends unconnected to your work life give you the opportunity to truly let your hair down, relax and let off steam. It is important not to let your friendships outside of work slide, as you never know when you may need them.

 **Support team exercise**

Summary

Your route to becoming the Go-To Expert is intrinsically linked to your ability to successfully lead, manage and develop your team. Building a successful team around you will free you from client work and enable you to focus on growing your client portfolio and practice as a whole.

In your role as a manager of people and leader of a team, you are responsible for making sure the client's work is completed to the right quality standard and within budget, whilst also building a team and individuals within it who are able and willing to achieve your goals for the team. To do this means you will need to allocate regular time with each team member to:

- review their work
- review their progress against their goals and objectives
- help develop them to acquire new skills and progress their careers.

As well as the team you work with on a day-to-day basis, you will need a support community around you. This support community will help you get to be the Go-To Expert on your terms.

Action points

Have a private conversation with each of your team members to find out what they like about their role and where they would like to progress their career. Then take action on this conversation.

1 Ask three people you trust and work with regularly for feedback on your abilities as a team leader. What will you do to act on their feedback to improve your abilities as a team leader?

2 Diarise regular conversations with your team members to find out how they are doing and what progress they are making on their personal objectives and current client assignments.

3 Book some time with your mentor and ask them how they learnt to manage people and lead teams. Then take action on what you have learnt.

4 If you are employed within a firm, ask a member of your firm, such as a member of the HR team, to sit in on a performance review that you run, to give you feedback and suggestions of what you could have done differently to be more effective.

5 Think about the teams you are either a member of or lead. What stage of team development are they at? What three actions will you take to increase the performance of each team?

6 Work with a coach to help improve your people management and leadership skills.

7 Volunteer to mentor a more junior member of your firm.

8 Look for role models, within and outside of your firm, who are recognised as Go-To Experts in their fields. Do research to find out how they have achieved their success. What can you learn from their experiences, and how will you apply this on your journey to becoming the Go-To Expert?

Further resources

We recommend these resources to help you build and lead a team.

BOOKS

- Blanchard, K., Zigarmi, P. and Zigarmi, D. (2000) *Leadership and the One Minute Manager*, London: HarperCollins
- Delong, T. J., Gabarro, J. J. and Lees, R. (2007) *When Professionals Have to Lead: A new model for high performance*, Boston, MA: Harvard Business School Press
- Kay, D. and Hinds, R. (2004) *A Practical Guide to Mentoring: Play an active and worthwhile part in the development of others, and improve your own skills in the process*, Chichester: How To Books, 4th edn
- Selden, B. (2010) *What to Do When You Become the Boss: How new managers become successful managers*, London: Headline
- Whitmore, J. (2009) *Coaching for Performance: GROWing human potential and purpose – the principles and practices of coaching and leadership*, London: Nicholas Brealey Publishing, 4th edn

WEBSITES

- Harvard Business Review Blogs **www.blogs.hbr.org**
- MENTOR – National Mentoring Partnership **www.mentoring.org/program_resources/library**
- How To Make Partner **www.howtomakepartner.com/category/managing-others**
- venture-Now **www.venture-now.com/category/blog/your-team**

15

How to keep your knowledge fresh

Topics covered in this chapter.

- How people learn and develop new skills and behaviours
- Stages of your development
- The importance of playing to your strengths
- How to identify gaps in your skill base
- How to keep your knowledge up to date

When you sell your time for money, your knowledge has a sell-by date. To remain as the Go-To Expert you will need to be investing continually in your technical and non-technical skill set. In this chapter we explore how you can build and develop both your technical and non-technical knowledge and skills that are needed on your journey to becoming the Go-To Expert.

"Learn from yesterday, live for today, hope for tomorrow. The important thing is not to stop questioning."

ALBERT EINSTEIN

How people learn and develop new skills and behaviours

People learn in different ways. There is no right way or wrong way to learn. By being aware of your preferred learning style you will learn and develop more quickly. For example, some people like to:

- read books and understand the theory
- watch and observe others
- get stuck in and just give it a go
- see a working example and understand how it will work in practice.

Think back to a time when you had to learn a new skill, how did you go about this?

Stages of your development

As you learn a new skill or behaviour, you go through four levels of increasing competence until you reach full competence. By recognising your stage of development, you can identify what you still need to do to fully master the skill or behaviour.

1 UNCONSCIOUS INCOMPETENCE

Think about when you first started to learn to drive a car. You were probably very enthusiastic about driving and thinking, 'How hard can it be to learn to drive?' This stage is characterised by enthusiasm and often unrealistic expectations of how easy it will be to gain the new skill.

2 CONSCIOUS INCOMPETENCE

At this stage you have started to learn the new skill and realise just how much you don't know or need to learn. Very often, this stage can be demoralising. Going back to the example of learning to drive, for most of us we were in a state of conscious incompetence for our first few lessons. Many of you may have picked this book up because you realised you needed more help than you first thought to become the Go-To Expert.

3 CONSCIOUS COMPETENCE

After a while we do start to learn the new skills and implement them. However, because they are so new to us, it takes a conscious effort to use them. For example, when you learnt to drive you used phrases like 'mirror, signal, manoeuvre' to remind you of what you needed to do every time you changed lane in traffic.

4 UNCONSCIOUS COMPETENCE

With practice, you get so good at doing a new skill that it becomes second nature and you no longer need to think about it. You just do it. As an experienced driver you no longer have to think about 'mirror, signal, manoeuvre' to change lanes, you just do it on autopilot.

"An investment in knowledge always pays the best interest."

BENJAMIN FRANKLIN

The importance of playing to your strengths

Case study 1
Abi

Abi started her career in tax compliance and, while she took pride in her work, she wasn't thriving and developing as quickly as her peers. She found the day-to-day work of checking and entering numbers into schedules and tax computation software to be boring and 'not her thing'. She was keen to develop her career to partner, so hired a career coach to help her progress. Her career coach helped her see that her strengths were working with people, rather than the routine technical work she was doing in tax compliance. She brainstormed options with her coach and asked her partner for a move into tax investigations. She soon found that the variety and the problem-solving element of the tax investigations work really suited her personality and natural preferences. Her aptitude and enthusiasm for the different type of work started to shine through and her career took off from that point.

How to identify gaps in your skill base

There are many tools available to you to help you identify your strengths and gaps, e.g. 360° feedback, psychometric profiling tools, internal firm assessment and development centres.

With our clients we use an executive insights tool called PROPHET© to help them recognise their strengths. Your PROPHET© profile determines what motivates you, then detects the way you think and make decisions. This then enables it to pinpoint the sorts of things that you will be good at. It then uses these insights to isolate the sort of role that would best suit your motivation and decisionmaking style. We use this information with our clients to tailor our service and coaching sessions to give the help they need from us to plug their weaknesses.

How to keep your knowledge up to date

Nothing ever stays the same in the world of professional services. The changing business environment, the speed of change and access to the internet means that current products, services and capabilities cannot guarantee a firm or individual's future business success. The only sources of long-term competitive advantage, for you, are the capacity to learn and to apply that knowledge and skills. Your future success as the Go-To Expert is reliant on you taking a disciplined approach to your self-development, rather than leaving it to chance or the rare moments of less activity.

Here are our tips for keeping your knowledge and skills up to date:

- always capture promptly, and share, what you have learnt winning or completing a piece of work
- have a filing system, ideally online, where you keep (and refer back to) interesting and relevant articles and documents
- combine business development activities, e.g. networking at a conference, with opportunities to learn
- identify the thought-leaders in your specialist area. Read their articles/blog, buy their books and attend their workshops, teleseminars, webinars and seminars

Your Decision-Making Style

This element of your profile describes the way you typically make decisions. The chart on the left indicates the extent to which your decision-making style is analytical - carefully assessing different options; systematic - following a very structured and logical thought process; inspired - very unstructured and free-thinking; or experimental - where you essentially make decisions by trial-and-error, learning from experience. The text on the right provides some customised commentary on the specific nature of your decision-making style.

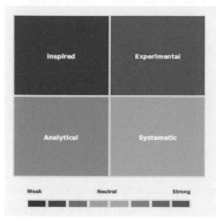

Your decision making style is Experimental and not Inspired.

You are likely to make decisions by testing, learning, trial-and-error. You tend not to make decisions by impulse, intuition, gut feel.

You are hands-on, restless, curious, independent. You relish opportunities to create change, show original thinking, have varied and unusual ideas.

At work, you prefer opportunities to make things happen, to be closely involved and hands-on. You dislike having to follow directions, keeping detailed records, bureaucracy, accepting when change is impossible. You may fear being tied down to rigid processes.

Inspired: These individuals are highly imaginative, dislike routine procedures and orderliness, and are highly flexible, accepting and responding easily to change. They are usually involved in multiple projects at the same time and learn well through discussion or sharing ideas. They tend to prefer a non-competitive atmosphere and assignments with room for interpretation. They dislike attending to details and giving exact answers, working within time limits and being corrected. They fear not being liked.

Experimental: These individuals are highly curious and enjoy investigating and hands-on experimentation. They like to discover their own way of doing things and must test things for themselves. They find possibilities to create change, have varied and unusual ideas and show original creativity. They tend to prefer a trial-and-error approach, hands-on experiences and open-ended activities. They are notorious for not reading directions and dislike keeping detailed records and accepting when change is impossible. They fear structure.

Analytical: These individuals gather information, analyse ideas and think in a structured and organised way. They strive for intellectual recognition and like to debate ideas and issues. They need a quiet environment to think and work, read avidly for information and enjoy research. They present ideas logically and tend to prefer working alone. They dislike expressing emotions, working cooperatively in groups, writing creatively and facing the unpredictable. They fear appearing foolish or uninformed.

Systematic: These individuals need and enjoy structured situations. They like clear and definitive directions. They also like things to be ordered and arranged in specific ways and are always busy, looking for constructive things to do. They are natural editors and can take anything and make it better. They tend to prefer order, stability, calm and to know the accepted way of doing something. They dislike making choices, open-ended assignments and "what-if" questions, and dealing with opposing views. They fear being wrong.

Figure 15.1 Part of a PROPHET© (ED86) profile

Source: www.optimaabr.com/prophet

- subscribe to the journal or magazine for your specialist area
- volunteer to be an early tester of new and emerging technology
- create time in your diary every month to acquire new knowledge relevant to your specialism.

Summary

To become and remain the Go-To Expert you will need to learn and apply daily new knowledge, skills and behaviours. Your personal and professional development is not something that should be left to chance, but woven into the way you do business.

Action points

1 Obtain a copy of Honey and Mumford's Learning Styles Questionnaire (**www.peterhoney.com**) to determine your preferred learning style. What have you learnt about yourself and how will you use this knowledge to improve your effectiveness?

2 If you work within a firm, ask your mentor, partner or manager what tools your firm has or uses to help people identify their development requirements. Then get permission to participate in these tools and act on your findings.

3 Ask for feedback on your performance at work from your clients, your peers and the people who work for you. An easy way to do this is to ask them for one thing you do well and one specific thing that you need to improve. Encourage them to be honest. Remember to listen to the feedback and take steps to improve your performance based on the feedback.

Further resources

To help you identify your strengths we recommend the following resource.

BOOK

- Buckingham, M. and Clifton, D. O. (2005) *Now, Discover Your Strengths: How to develop your talents and those of the people you manage*, London: Pocket Books

16

Building your plan and making it happen

Topics covered in this chapter.

- How to build your one-page Go-To Expert business plan.
- Your next steps.

Well done for reaching the final chapter of the book! This is probably the most important chapter because it is the one that will help you translate what you have been reading into real, tangible things that you will do to make a real difference to the size and shape of your client portfolio. After all, don't you owe it to you, your family and people around you to enjoy the status and rewards that come with being the Go-To Expert?

It's one thing to read a book on becoming the Go-To Expert, it's another thing entirely to act on what is contained in this book and use it to become one. As we stated in the Introduction, our clients have tested and used successfully all the ideas, tips and techniques contained in this book. Therefore, next get out a pen and download your copy of the Go-To Expert Workbook from **www.joinedupnet-working.com/the-go-to-expert-workbook** and commit to becoming the Go-To Expert. Surely, after all the time you have taken to get this far in your career and business, don't you deserve to be recognised, valued, booked and in demand for doing what you love?

> *"We are drowning in information, while starving for wisdom. The world henceforth will be run by synthesizers, people able to put together the right information at the right time, think critically about it, and make important choices wisely."*
>
> E.O. WILSON

Brian is known as the Go-To Expert for crofting law. He comes from Shetland, which is one of the crofting counties in Scotland. When he was working as a trainee and assistant solicitor in Glasgow, he had friends, family and referrals from Shetland asking him to do legal work for them. This resulted in Brian needing to learn about crofting law – it's not a subject taught at law school or university.

When Brian joined the Crofting Law Group in 1994, he realised that he was one of the group's youngest members. He took an active interest in the group's activities and religiously attended their annual conferences. Brian is currently the Honourable Secretary of the group.

In 1999, when Brian set up his own law firm, he consciously started to build up his visibility and profile as the Go-To Expert for crofting law. He has done this via a mixture of writing, speaking, seminars, lecturing and social media – e.g., in 1999 he registered the web domain **www.croftinglaw.com**; in 2009 he created his first crofting law video for YouTube as well as starting a crofting law Twitter account; in 2013 he started blogging about crofting law.

He regularly, and proactively, speaks about crofting law – e.g., in 2009, he organised a series of lectures on crofting law for Strathclyde University and, in 2012, ran seminars for crofters in North Uist and Benbecula; in 2012 and 2013, he attended the Black Isle Show with a marquee dedicated to crofting law. He has also produced a brochure on crofting law to hand out at any event he does for crofters.

As well as his crofting law blog, Brian has written numerous articles for the *Journal of the Law Society of Scotland*, *The Firm*, and the *Island News & Advertiser* (the Shetland Islands local newspaper that is read by crofters). He has collaborated widely with others in the industry and, as a result, his firm provides a legal helpline to the Scottish Crofting Federation's members.

He has been recognised as the expert on crofting law by the Scottish Parliament. Tweets and blogs by Brian have been referred to in Scottish Parliamentary debates on crofting law. He sits on the Cross Party Group on Crofting within the Scottish Parliament and is a member of the Crofting Group of Scottish Land and Estates.

Although he is a specialist in crofting law, his firm deals with many of the other legal services that crofters also need, from the highly specialist fishing law for the salmon and mussel farmers on the Shetland Islands to the more generalist family law services.

As a result of the work Brian has done over the last 15 years to grow his profile and visibility as the Go-To Expert for crofting law, his legal business has thrived. He finds that new business consistently comes to him and his firm via his website, blog, Twitter and referrals from other professionals. In the last few years, he has recruited two solicitors with a specialism in crofting law to cope with the demand for his services and Inksters has opened two new offices in addition to its Glasgow main office.

How to build your one-page Go-To Expert business plan

Regardless of whether you run your own practice or are employed by a professional practice, you will need a 12-month plan to help you grow your part of the practice. We tend to use a simple one-page Go-To Expert business plan with our clients. In the Go-To Expert Workbook there is a template for you to use to write your one-page Go-To Expert business plan.

MISSION & VISION	• Become the Go-To Expert accountant for solicitor's practices in 50-mile radius of office • Grow the practice so we are a £3 million, 3 partner practice • Generate yearly £150,000 take-home income
OBJECTIVES	• Increase GRF from £1 m to £1.2 m • Add £20,000 GRF each month • Increase headcount from 20 to 25 • Increase fees from existing clients by 5% • Increase average client engagement size from £3,000 to £3,500
PROJECTS & STRATEGIES	• Rebuild website so our specialism of solicitor practices is clearly shown • Build social media capability in firm and get at least 50% of firm active on social media • Research with existing solicitor clients what help they would like from their account
MARKETING	• Write weekly blog post focused on solicitor practices • Train all the fee earners to develop business via their network • Write monthly report/white paper/long article of interest to solicitors' practices • Run client satisfaction survey • Make sure all clients are spoken to at least quarterly
PEOPLE	• Recruit experienced senior manager who has a following and desire for partnership • Run staff satisfaction survey – and act on results • Recruit four trainees or part-qualified members of staff

Figure 16.1 A one-page Go-To Expert business plan

Use these questions to help you complete your one-page Go-To Expert business plan.

PERSONAL MISSION AND VISION

- How do you visualise your client portfolio in the future?
- How will your client portfolio help you have the lifestyle you want and further your business and/or career ambitions?
- What utilisation do you want to personally achieve? What work do you want to be able to provide for the rest of your firm?

OBJECTIVES

What must you achieve with your client portfolio within one year to be successful?

- Revenue? Profit? Cost of sales?
- Size of mailing list? Follower numbers? Website traffic?
- Percentage of revenue split between service/product lines?

PROJECTS AND STRATEGIES

What key projects or strategies must you deliver in the year to help build your client portfolio?

- Marketing campaigns?
- Deliver key pieces of IP?
- Increase lead generation?

MARKETING

- Who is your niche market? How will you reach it?
- What channels to market will you focus on?
- What resources (time and money) will you spend on marketing in the year?
- How will you keep prospects, leads and clients within your sales and marketing funnel?

PEOPLE

- Who are the key people within and external to your firm?
- What are their responsibilities or what do you need them to do?
- What will you do? What will you delegate? What will you outsource to others?

"Know what you want to do, hold the thought firmly, and do every day what should be done, and every sunset will see you that much nearer to your goal."

ELBERT HUBBARD

Your next steps

We've come to the end of the book, so there is only really one last action for you – *implement* your Go-To Expert business plan, starting right now. (Yes, right now!) Drop us an email (heather@excedia.co.uk or jon@excedia.co.uk) telling us about the progress you make.

Index

motivation 4, 241–3, 247, 254
  career progression 241–2, 246–7
  goal-setting 6, 9, 90
  interesting and challenging work
    241
  networking 91
  niches 21, 29, 31
  public speaking 130–1, 138
  publishing 111, 113, 122, 124
  skill gaps 254
  valued, feeling 241, 242

name badges 54
national press 154
nerves, conquering 140–1
networking 87–107
  A-, B- and C- system 94–100, 102,
    106–7
  audits 89, 91–3
  building the network 89, 94–8, 106
  case studies xxvi–xxvii, 6, 21, 33, 91,
    97, 172
  collaborate level 96
  connect level 96
  content plans 100, 107
  credibility statements and stories 43,
    101
  deepening relationships 94, 98–100,
    106–7
  effectiveness 87–8, 92–3
  engage level 96
  Excedia 5-level relationship model
    95–7
  face-to-face meetings 197
  finding people to add to network
    89, 93–4, 96
  five-step process 87, 89–100
  goals 89, 90–1
  identify level 96
  inner circle level 96–7
  keeping-in-touch strategy 199
  maintaining relationships 89, 94,
    98–100
  maps 92–3, 101, 106
  public speaking 130, 145
  referrals/recommendations 87–8, 90,
    94–6, 100–6, 145
  regular communication 90, 95, 100
  relationship plans 95, 98, 99, 107
  routine 105, 106
  seminars, selling 172, 175

SERVICE framework (Excedia) 87,
    101–5, 106
  social media 88
  sound bites 101
  strategy, building your 89–100, 106
  Twitter 90, 91, 95
  valuable content, sharing 100
newsletters 30, 67–9, 73, 82, 104,
    199–200
niche, determination of 13–26
  boredom, fear of 20–1
  case studies xxii–xxiii, xxvi–xxvii, 15,
    20–1, 34–5
  client churn, minimising 19, 25
  commitment, importance of 16–19,
    101, 229, 230
  differentiation 17
  emotional connection 16, 20, 23,
    24–5
  finding your niche 21–3, 24–5
  growth 17, 25, 229, 230
  marketing 16, 20, 29–30, 263
  more than one niche, having 20
  premium fees, charging 18
  prospects/potential leads 17–18
  referrals and recommendations 16,
    101
  resistance to adoption of niche
    19–21
  specialisation 21, 24
  tailoring services to clients 17–18
  turning business away, fear of 19
no win, no fee arrangements 35
non-traditional business models 33–4

OAL (objective, agenda, logistics
    meeting planner) 208–10
one-pagers
  business plans 261–2
  credentials documents 50–1, 142
  public relations 156, 168
  public speaking 52, 142, 144, 147
  relationship hooks 50–1
online publication 25, 152–3, 167
outsourcing 142, 238, 263
overexposure 157

packaging services 32–4
pain points 30–1, 36, 42, 59, 79, 104,
    183
partners 103–4, 121, 180–1, 232–3

public speaking (*continued*)
audience analysis 132
bureaus or agencies 145, 146, 148
case studies 142, 145
closing, writing the 134–5
content speakers 131, 132–3
contract 142
credibility statements 52
designing speeches 131–6, 140
dress 139
eye contact 137
fees 130
free or reduced rates, speaking for
146–7
hooks 133, 135
impact, delivering a speech with
137–41
index cards 136
instructions for organisers 142, 144
interactive exercises 133
introduction for conference hosts
142, 144, 148
introductions 133
keynote speeches 129, 130–1, 133,
136, 141, 142, 143, 148
kits, content of speaker 52–3, 142–4,
146, 147–8
marketing mix, as part of 129–30,
147
maximum content 132–3
motivational speakers 131
nerves and confidence 137–8, 140–1
networking 130, 145
one-pager or speaker sheets 52, 142,
144, 147
open loops 134
opening, writing the 133–4
pauses 137
practice, importance of 140, 141
presenting, distinguished from
130–1
public relations 166
publishing 109
question and answer sessions 130,
133, 135, 139–40
referrals and recommendations 145,
147
securing engagements 145–7
show reels/video clips of you
speaking 52, 142, 143, 146, 147,
148

sponsors of conferences 133
stand, how you 138
standard keynotes 136, 142, 148
storytelling, medium of 130, 133–4
summaries 135
testimonials 142, 143, 148
training 36, 141
transitions, writing 135, 136
visual aids and slides 130, 131, 133,
136, 142, 144
voice 138
websites 148
publishing 109–26 *see also* book
proposal, writing the
agents 118, 120
benefits of writing a book 109–11
bestseller, what constitutes a 111
challenges of writing a book 109,
111–12
charge-out rates 110
co-authors 121
conference organisers 110
credibility statements 109–10, 113,
125
editors 112, 117–18, 119, 121
five steps 112–22, 125
interviews, recording and
transcribing 122
marshalling thoughts 110–11
Microsoft Word 120
pitches 112–17, 119
positioning for your book 113–14
production team 117–19
professional speakers 109
profits 111
project managers 117
publishers 116–17, 119–20, 123
self-publishing 121, 123–5
status and authority 109–11
time issues 109–11, 121–2
writing the book 120–2
pushiness 196

question and answer sessions 130, 133,
135, 139–40

radio, getting on 164–5
reasons for becoming a Go-To Expert
3–10
referrals/recommendations 87–8, 90,
94–6, 100–6